Malware Narratives

Introduction

Revised Version

Dmitry Vostokov

Software Diagnostics Services

Published by OpenTask, Republic of Ireland

OpenTask books and magazines are available through booksellers and distributors worldwide. For further information or comments, send requests to press@opentask.com.

A CIP catalog record for this book is available from the British Library.

ISBN-l3: 978-1-912636-52-5 (Paperback)

First printing, 2013
Revision 2 (July 2015)
Revision 3 (March 2023)

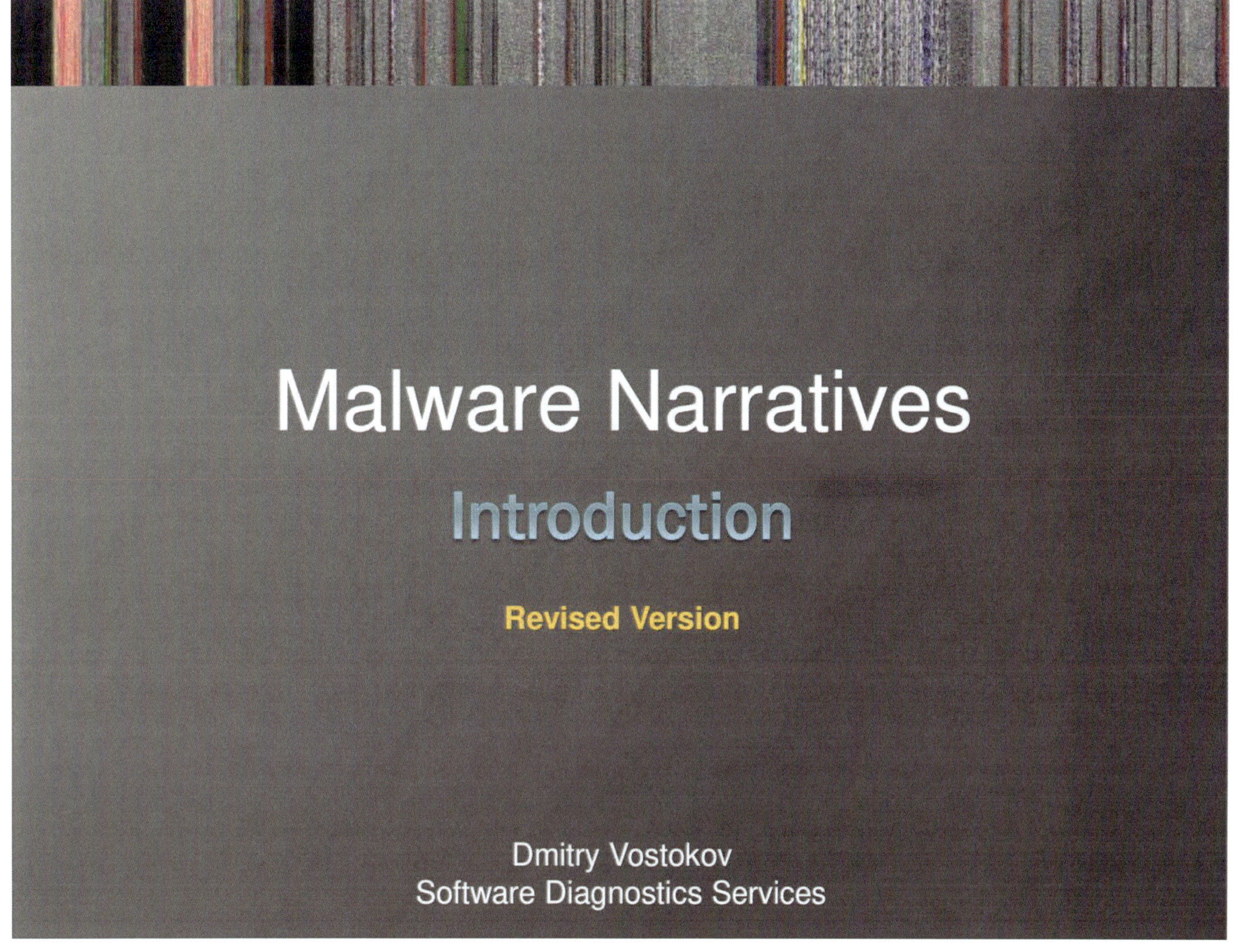

Hello Everyone, my name is Dmitry Vostokov, and I introduce today a software narratological approach to malware analysis of software traces and logs. I decided to keep this presentation short and as simple as possible. If anything needs to be added or modified in the future, I create another version of it.

Facebook:
https://www.facebook.com/SoftwareDiagnosticsServices

Linkedin:
https://www.linkedin.com/company/software-diagnostics-services

Twitter:
https://twitter.com/DumpAnalysis

Prerequisites

Interest in software diagnostics and malware analysis

These prerequisites are very simple, and I suppose you all, like me, enjoy diagnosing malware and often going side-by-side with corresponding software problems.

Why?

- Communication language

- Malware diagnostics as software diagnostics

- Big DA+TA (Dump Artifacts + Trace Artifacts)

Why do we advocate a different approach to traditional log analysis? First, we need a unified communication language in the context of general software diagnostics, and second, an approach to tackling big DA+TA that, in our context, means memory dump and trace artifacts. The proliferation of mobile technologies might seem to be making memory dump analysis redundant, but the memory size is ever-increasing for mobile and embedded devices, and software traces ad logs are just a form of memory dumps. Also, don't forget about massive cloud systems.

Software Diagnostics

A discipline studying signs of software structure and behavior in software execution artifacts (such as memory dumps, software and network traces and logs) using systemic and pattern-oriented analysis methodologies.

First, I would like to remind you of a definition of software diagnostics we put forward in one of our previous webinars. We also use words such as "trace" and "log" interchangeably. So you see that malware detection and associated software behavior fall under the definition of software diagnostics.

Pattern-Driven Software Diagnostics:

https://www.dumpanalysis.org/introduction-pattern-driven-diagnostics

Systemic Software Diagnostics:

https://www.dumpanalysis.org/introduction-systemic-software-diagnostics

Pattern-Based Software Diagnostics:

https://www.dumpanalysis.org/introduction-pattern-based-software-diagnostics

Diagnostics Pattern

A common recurrent identifiable problem together with a set of recommendations and possible solutions to apply in a specific context.

Next, we would like to mention a definition of a software diagnostics pattern. There are some differences from a usual definition of a pattern from software construction, such as architectural and design patterns. The difference is that often upon a diagnostic encounter, we provide recommendations and possible solutions instead of just problem solutions. Recommendations may include immediate actions, for example, upon detecting suspicious activity.

Pattern Orientation

Pattern-driven

- Finding patterns in software artefacts
- Using checklists and pattern catalogs

Pattern-based

- Pattern catalog evolution
- Catalog packaging and delivery

So you see that software diagnostics is about patterns and pattern recognition. Let's say it is pattern-oriented and includes pattern-based and pattern-driven parts. Pattern-driven is about the diagnostics process, and pattern-based is about the pattern life cycle. We start with the pattern-driven part first.

Catalog Classification

- **By abstraction**

  Meta-patterns

- **By artifact type**

  Software Log*   Memory Dump   Network Trace*

- **By story type**

  Problem Description   Software Disruption   UI Problem

- **By intention**

  Malware

In pattern-driven analysis, we use pattern catalogs. Catalogs can be classified by abstraction, for example, as software diagnostics meta-patterns which are patterns of software diagnostics itself, by the type of software execution artifacts, such as software traces and logs, memory dumps and network traces, by story type, such as by problem descriptions, by software disruptions, and by user interface problems. Also, we can separate patterns by intention, such as malware (with unintentional patterns, the rest, all grouped as Victimware). In this presentation, we only consider software logs and network traces.

Meta-patterns:
https://www.dumpanalysis.org/blog/index.php/2012/06/09/patterns-of-software-diagnostics-part-1/

Software Log:
https://www.dumpanalysis.org/blog/index.php/trace-analysis-patterns/

Memory Dump:
https://www.dumpanalysis.org/blog/index.php/crash-dump-analysis-patterns/

Network Trace:
https://www.dumpanalysis.org/blog/index.php/2012/07/19/network-trace-analysis-patterns-part-1/

Problem Description:
https://www.dumpanalysis.org/blog/index.php/2012/03/11/software-problem-description-patterns-part-1/

Software Disruption:
https://www.dumpanalysis.org/blog/index.php/2013/01/12/software-disruption-patterns-part-1/

UI Problem:
https://www.dumpanalysis.org/blog/index.php/user-interface-problem-analysis-patterns/

Malware:
https://www.dumpanalysis.org/blog/index.php/malware-analysis-patterns/

Malware

Software that uses planned alteration of structure and behavior of software to serve malicious purposes.

Because our presentation is related to malware, we provide its definition: software that uses planned alteration of structure and behavior of software to serve malicious purposes. Notice the recursive character of that definition that includes self-modifying malware and also rootkits where a malicious purpose is to conceal.

Memory Analysis Patterns

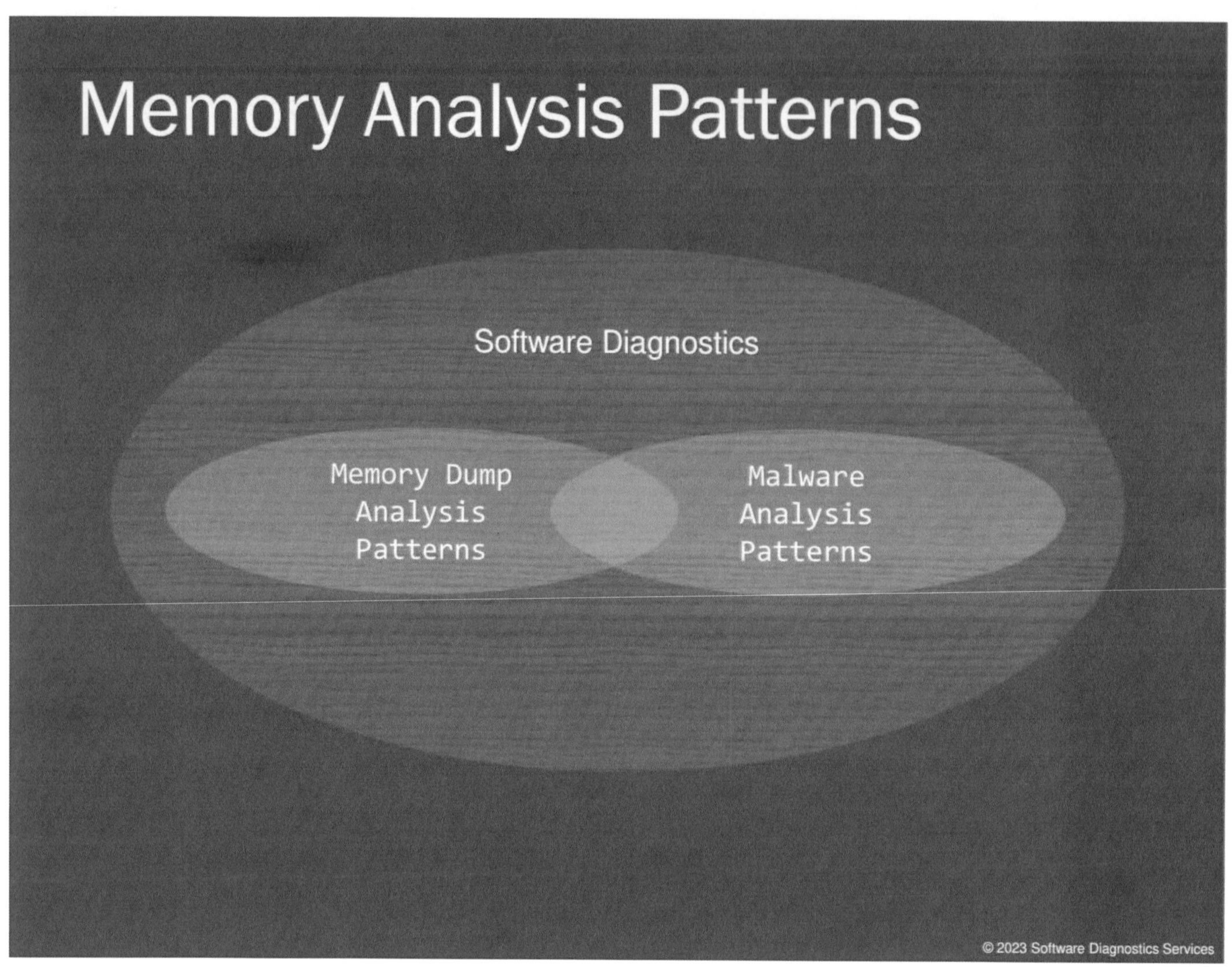

Before we proceed to software traces and logs, I would like to say a few words about memory and memory dumps. Some time ago, we created a separate malware pattern catalog for memory analysis. Due to the intentional nature of malware, there is only a partial overlap of them; for example, **Out-of-Module Pointer** (a pointer in a structure is considered malicious if it points outside the module code range) is considered to be malware specific.

Traces and Logs

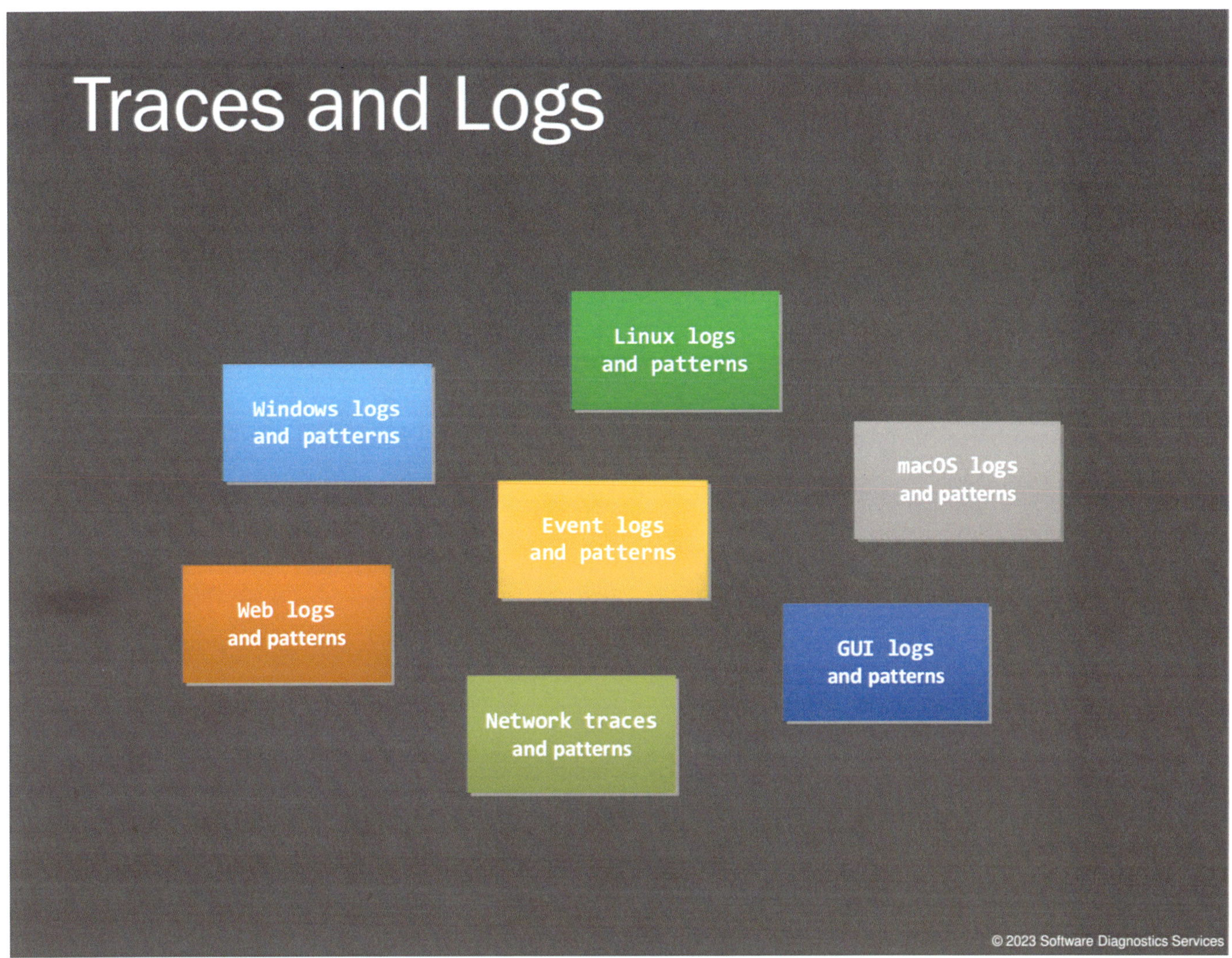

In addition to live memory and memory snapshot artifacts, software diagnostics also analyzes various software traces and logs. There are so many of them with different formats, from different OS, and product-specific information.

Trace and Log Patterns

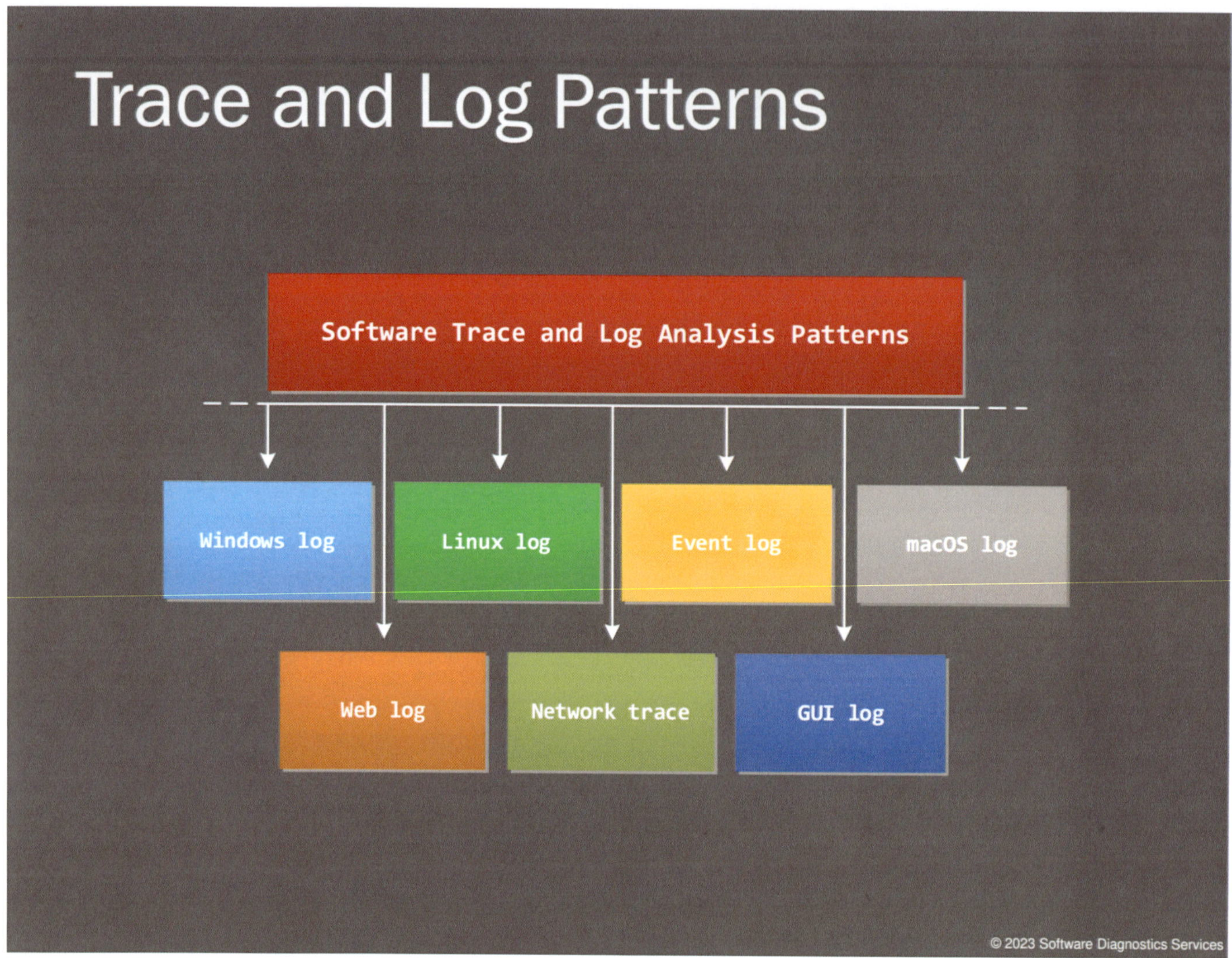

A unifying approach was needed for a pattern catalog. The solution would use the common structure of all these logs and associated patterns.

Software Narrative

A temporal sequence of events related to software execution.

We, therefore, considered using narratology, the discipline that studies various narrative forms such as stories, novels, and movies, because all these logs have the same unified narrative structure, such as events ordered by time.

Narrative Taxonomy

- Incident stories
- Software traces and logs
- Malware analysis stories

There are several types of narratives related to malware analysis. In this presentation, we only limit ourselves to software traces and logs as stories of software execution and communication.

Malware Narrative Patterns

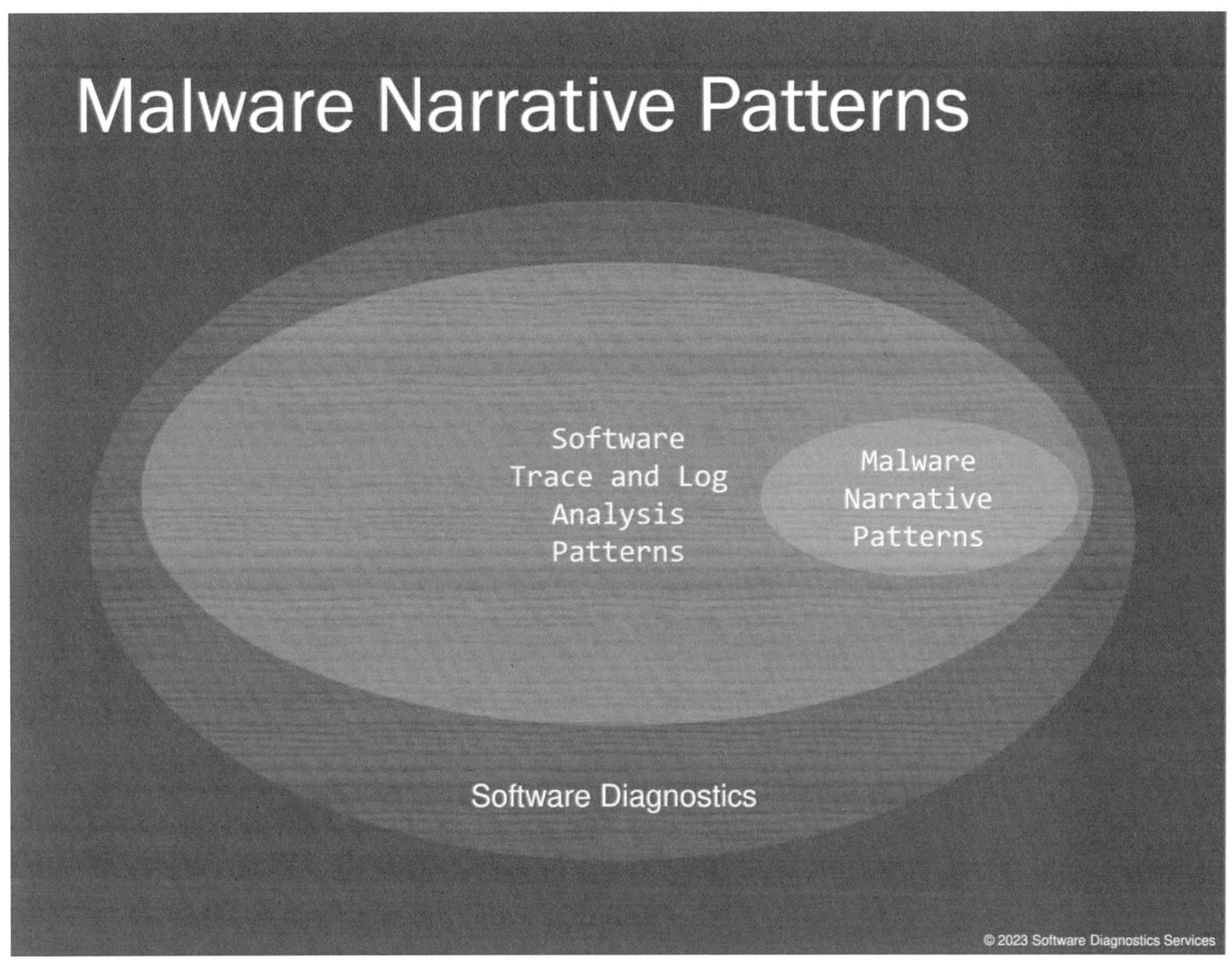

By malware narrative patterns, we consider a subset of software trace and log analysis patterns because the same logs can also be used to analyze abnormal software behavior, troubleshooting, and debugging, and they all have the same underlying narratological structure.

Software Log

- A sequence of formatted messages
- Arranged by time
- A narrative story

What is a software trace or log, actually? For our purposes, it is just a sequence of formatted messages sent from running software, for example, an event log or intercepted and formatted API requests such as a log from the Process Monitor tool or even a network trace. They are usually arranged by time and can be considered as a software narrative story.

Minimal Trace Graphs

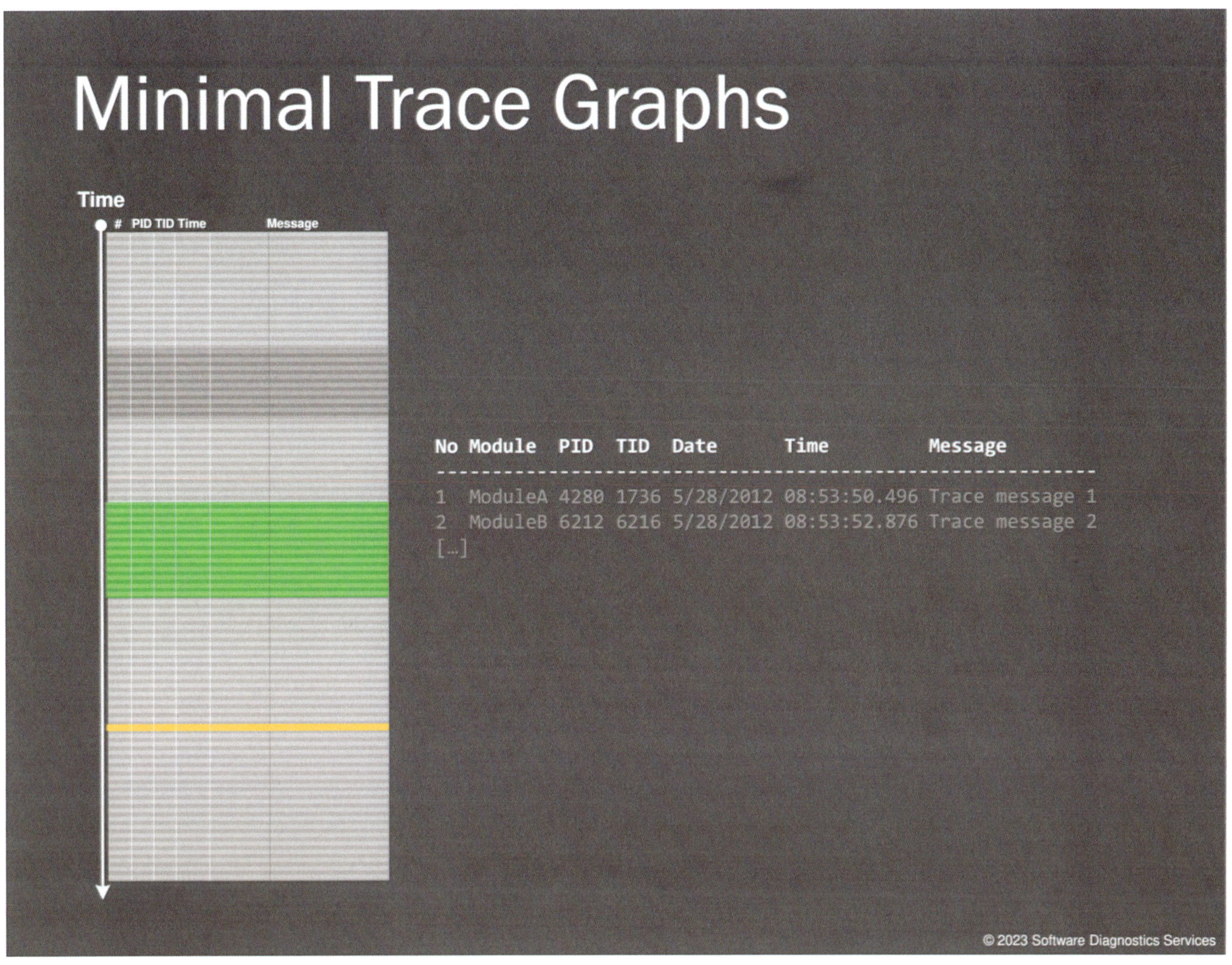

In order to illustrate log analysis patterns graphically, we use the simplified, abstracted pictorial representation of a typical software log. It has all essential features such as message number, time, PID, TID, and message text.

Pattern-Driven Analysis

Diagnostic Pattern: a common recurrent identifiable problem together with a set of recommendations and possible solutions to apply in a specific context.

Diagnostic Problem: a set of indicators (symptoms, signs) describing a problem.

Diagnostic Analysis Pattern: a common recurrent analysis technique and method of diagnostic pattern identification in a specific context.

Diagnostics Pattern Language: common names of diagnostic and diagnostic analysis patterns. The same language for any operating system: Windows, macOS, Linux, ...

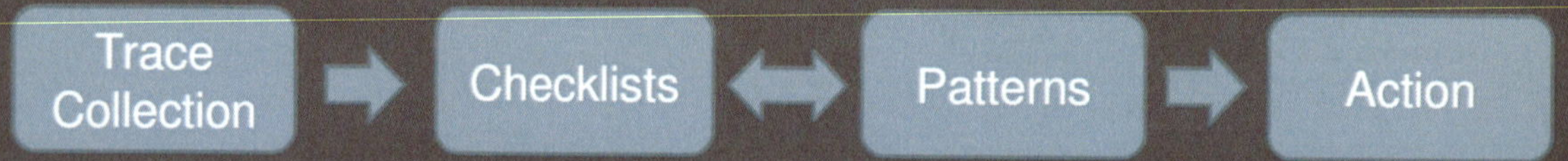

Checklist: http://www.dumpanalysis.org/blog/index.php/2011/03/10/software-trace-analysis-checklist/
Patterns: http://www.dumpanalysis.org/blog/index.php/trace-analysis-patterns/

A few words about logs, checklists, and patterns. Software log analysis is usually an analysis of a text for the presence of patterns. Here checklists can be very useful.

Checklist (also available in *Memory Dump Analysis Anthology, Volume 6, page 297*):
https://www.dumpanalysis.org/blog/index.php/2011/03/10/software-trace-analysis-checklist/

Patterns (also available in *Trace, Log, Text, Narrative, Data: An Analysis Pattern Reference for Information Mining, Diagnostics, Anomaly Detection, Fifth Edition*, see **Resources** page at the end of this book):
https://www.dumpanalysis.org/blog/index.php/trace-analysis-patterns/

Pattern-Based Analysis

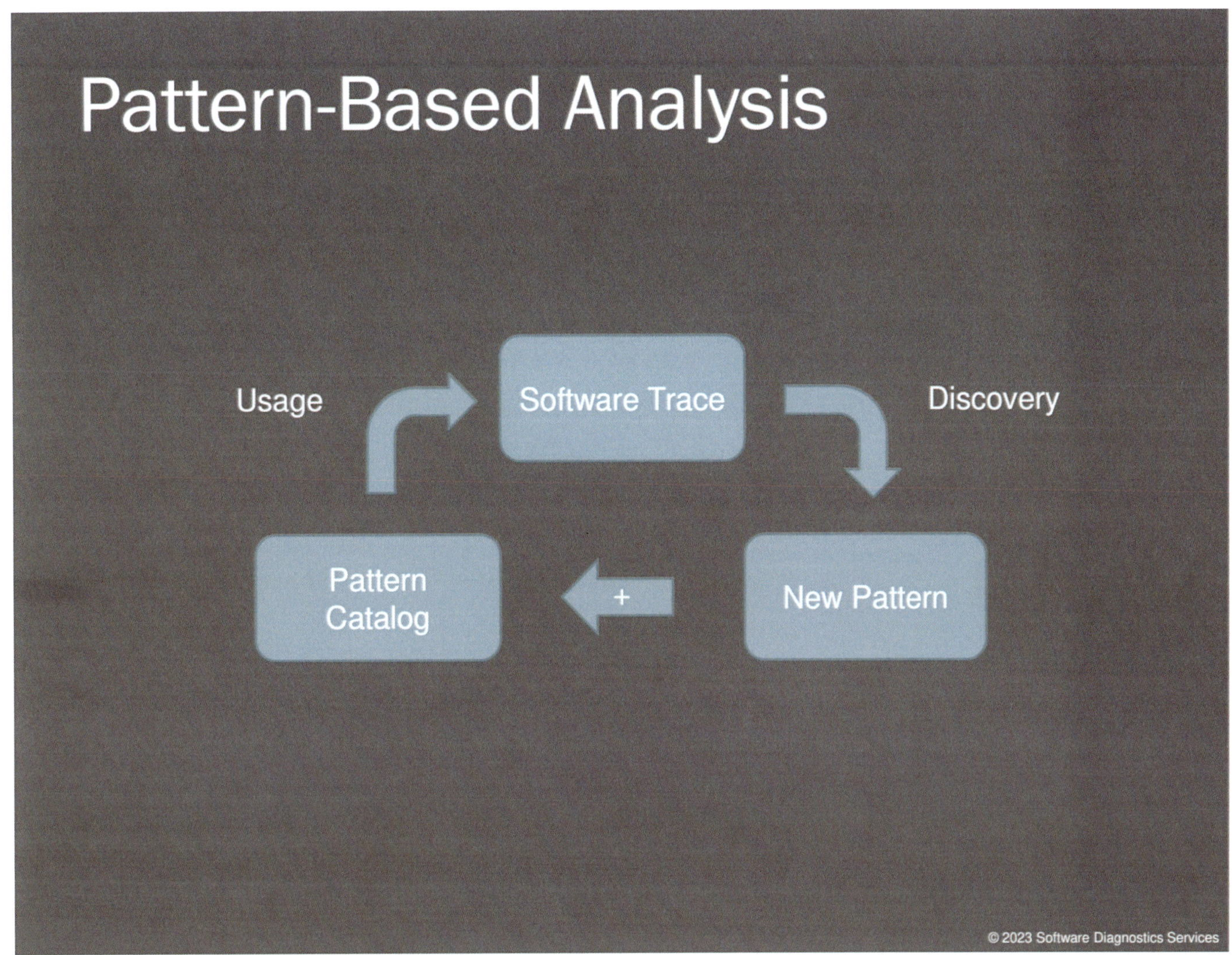

Pattern catalogs are rarely fixed. New patterns are constantly discerned or refined. For example, while preparing the first version of this book, I found yet another missing pattern and added it to the trace analysis pattern catalog.

Pattern Classification

- Vocabulary
- Error
- Trace as a Whole
- Large Scale
- Activity
- Message
- Block
- Trace Set

Recently all software trace and log analysis patterns (which were numbered almost 70 at the time of the first version and are now numbered almost 230 at the time of this third version) were classified into several categories. The vocabulary category consists of patterns related to the problem description. The error category covers general error distribution patterns. This classification also considers races as wholes, their large-scale structure, activity patterns, patterns related to individual trace message structure, patterns related to the collection of messages (the so-called blocks), and finally, patterns related to several traces and logs as a collection of artifacts from software incidents. Because malware detection and analysis is only a part of general software diagnostics, we selected only a few patterns from these categories as relevant. Of course, all this selection will be revised in the future version of this classification.

Reference and Course

- Catalog

Software Trace and Log Analysis Patterns

- Free reference graphical slides

Accelerated-Software-Trace-Analysis-Part1-Public.pdf

- Training course

Accelerated Software Trace Analysis

Most of the patterns are very intuitive if you analyze logs and traces. Here I provided a few links; after you download a presentation, you can follow them. Although most pattern examples are for the Windows platform, they are really a platform and product independent.

Software Log Analysis Patterns:
https://www.dumpanalysis.org/blog/index.php/trace-analysis-patterns/

Free reference graphical slides:
https://www.patterndiagnostics.com/Training/Accelerated-Software-Trace-Analysis-Part1-Public.pdf

Training course:
https://www.patterndiagnostics.com/accelerated-software-trace-analysis-part1

Vocabulary Patterns

- Basic Facts*
- Vocabulary Index

* patterns marked with yellow color are most likely to be useful for malware detection and analysis

The first block of patterns contains vocabulary patterns related to an incident description from a user's point of view. A typical log is a detailed software narrative that might include lots of irrelevant information with useful messages like needles in a haystack. However, it is usually accompanied by an incident description that lists essential facts. Therefore, the first task of any log analysis is to check the presence of **Basic Facts** (or it is usually called *Supporting Materials*) in the log. If they are not visible or do not correspond, then the trace was possibly not recorded during the incident or was taken from a different computer or under different conditions.

Error Patterns

- Error Message
- Exception Stack Trace
- False Positive Error
- Periodic Error
- Error Distribution

The next block contains error patterns related to error and failure messages either explicitly stating that there is an error or doing that indirectly via error code, abnormal function return value, or NT status values in the failure range. These patterns may be relevant when some malware causes some malfunction (the so-called victimware) or itself experiences abnormal behavior. We do not cover them here.

Trace as a Whole

- Partition
- Circular Trace
- Message Density
- Message Current
- Trace Acceleration
- No Trace Metafile
- Empty Trace
- Missing Module
- Guest Module
- Truncated Trace
- Visibility Limit
- Sparse Trace

The third block of patterns contains patterns related to a software trace or log as a whole. We ignore trace message contents and treat all messages statistically. Here we see only one pattern relevant to malware analysis specifically, and it is called **Guest Module**.

Guest Component

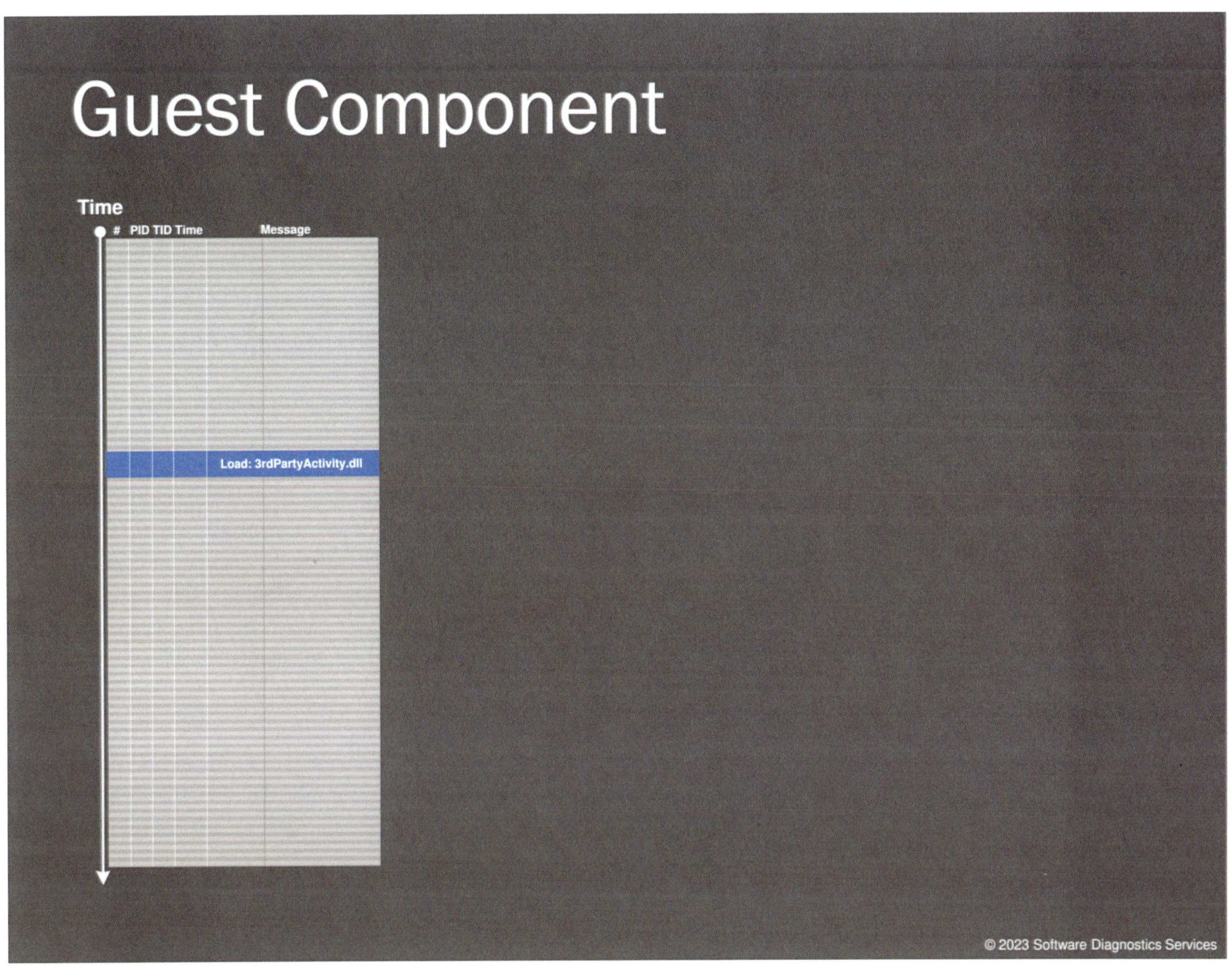

Often, when comparing normal, expected, and suspicious traces, we can get clues by looking at module load events. For example, when we see an unexpected module load event in our suspicious trace, this may prompt us to investigate it further.

Large Scale Patterns

- **Characteristic Message Block**
- Background Components
- **Foreground Components**
- Layered Periodization
- **Focus of Tracing**
- Event Sequence Order
- Trace Frames

The fourth block consists of large-scale log patterns. They are about the coarse grain structure of software traces and logs where the division unit is often a module or some high-level functionality. Here we would like to highlight 3 patterns that make sense for malware detection and analysis: **Characteristic Message Block**, **Foreground Components**, and **Focus of Tracing**.

Characteristic Message Block

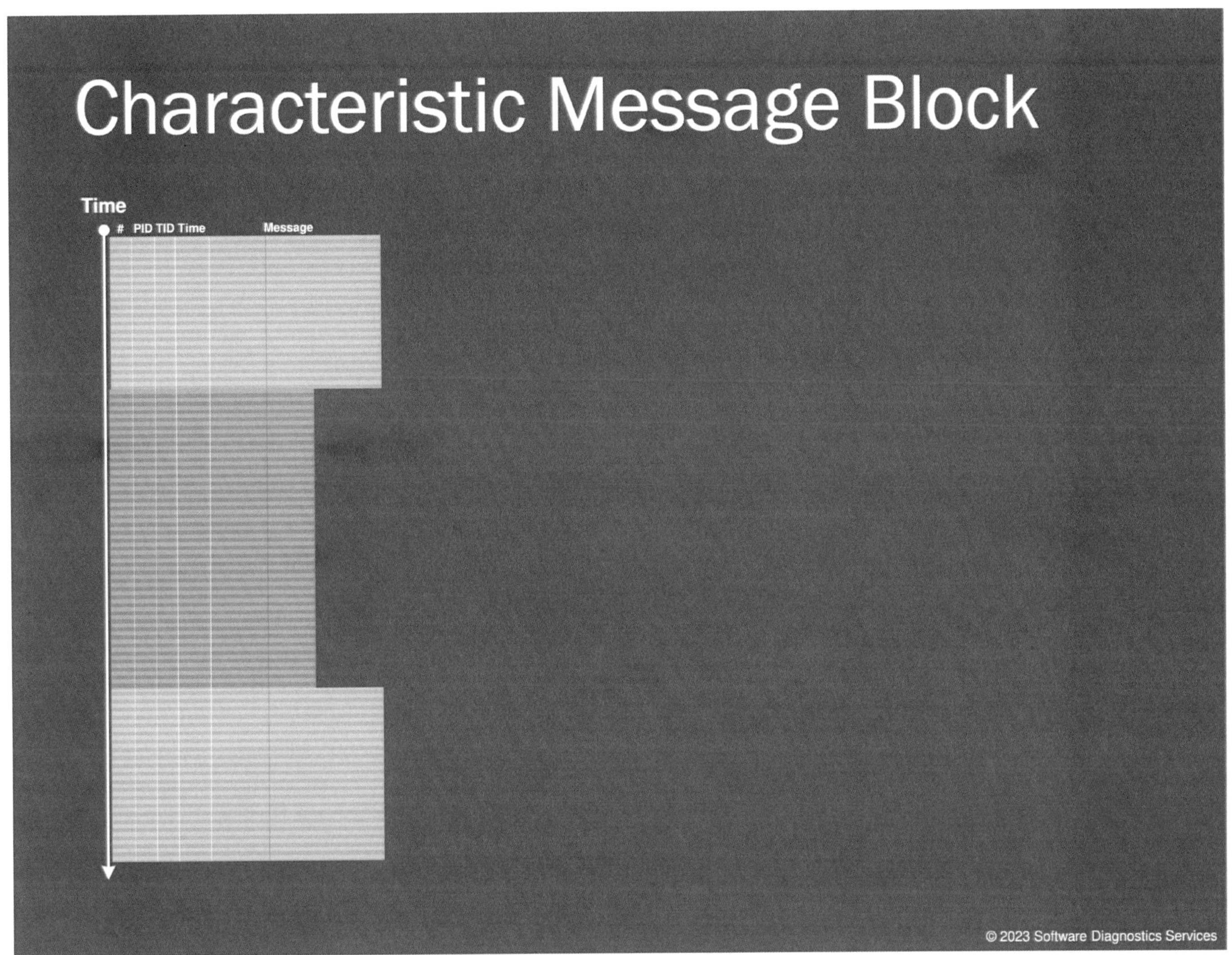

Textual representations can also be viewed from a bird's eye perspective. Irregularities in formatting make it easier to see the coarse blocked structure of a software trace or log.

Foreground Components

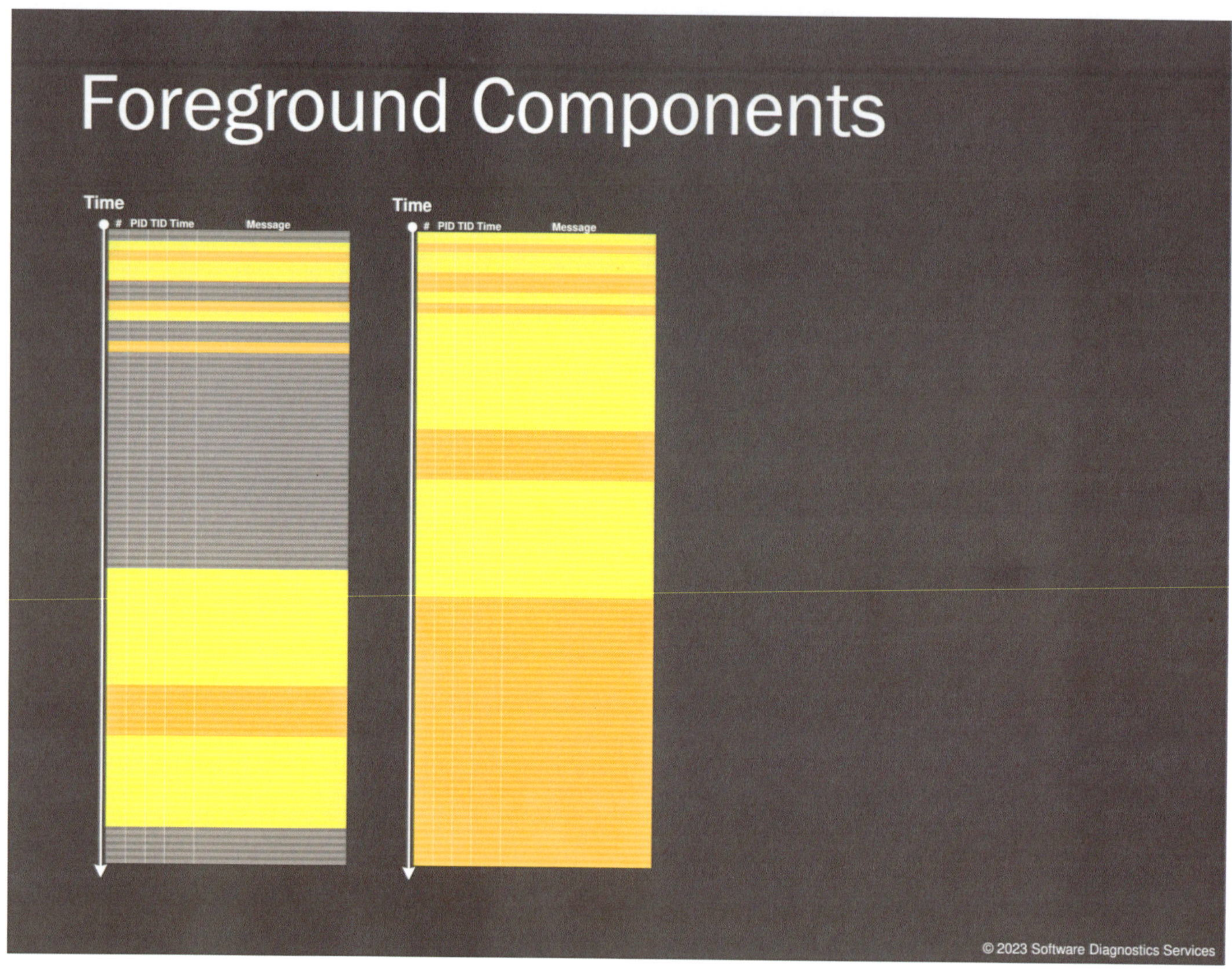

Log and trace viewers such as Process Monitor and network analysis tools can filter out (or exclude) background component messages and present only foreground modules (that we call **module** or **component foregrounding**). Here background modules can be considered as noise to filter out. Of course, this process is iterative, and parts of what once was foreground become background and candidates for further filtering.

Focus of Tracing

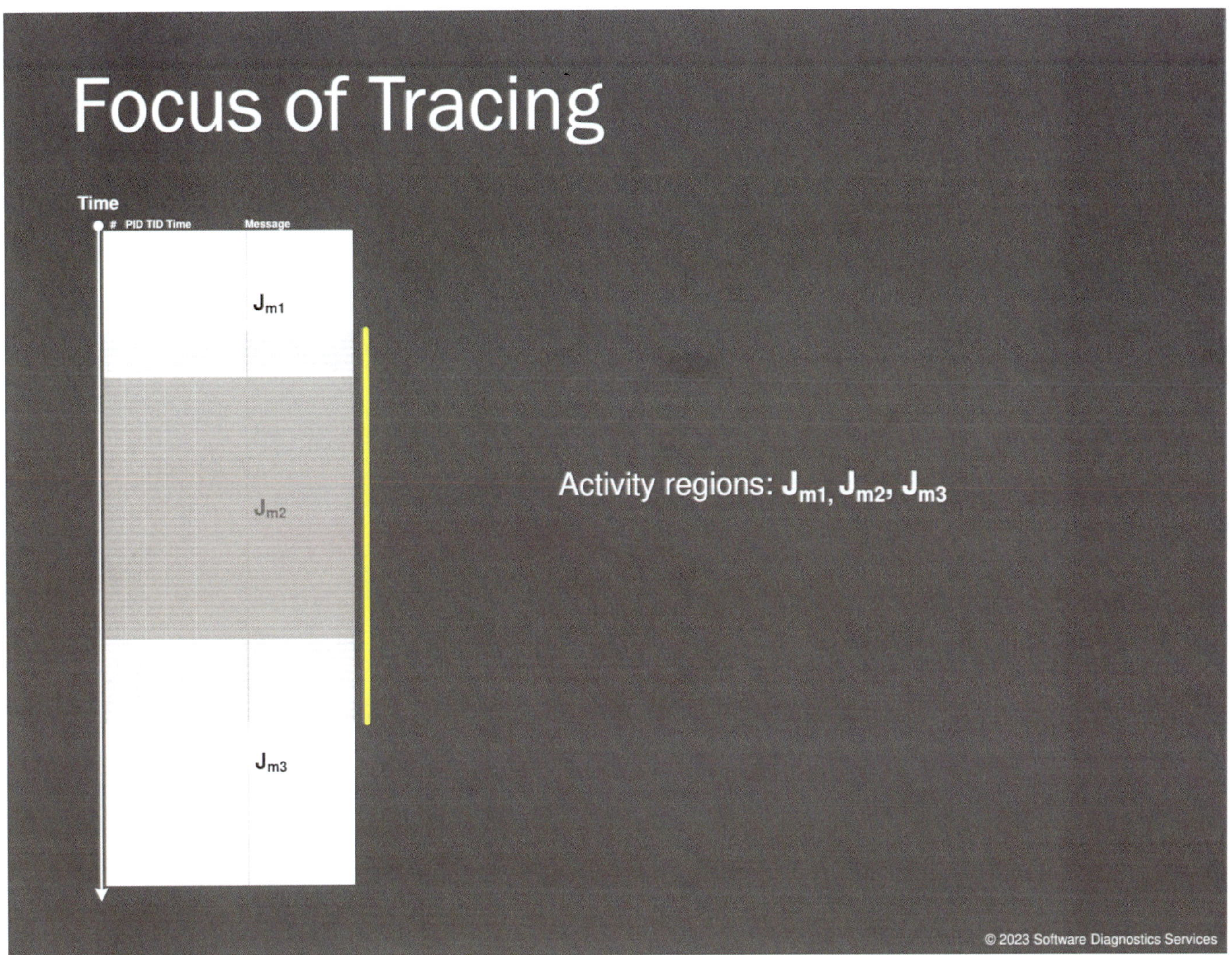

A software trace or log consists of the so-called **Activity Regions** with syntactical and visual aspects of log analysis, whereas **Focus of Tracing** brings attention to changing semantics of log message flow. Here is a graphical illustration of this pattern where the tracing focus region spans 3 regions of activity.

Activity Patterns

- Thread of Activity
- Adjoint Thread of Activity
- No Activity
- Activity Region
- Discontinuity
- Time Delta
- Glued Activity
- Break-in Activity
- Resume Activity
- Data Flow

The fifth block of patterns relates to various software activities we see in logs and traces. Most of them involve time dependency.

Thread of Activity

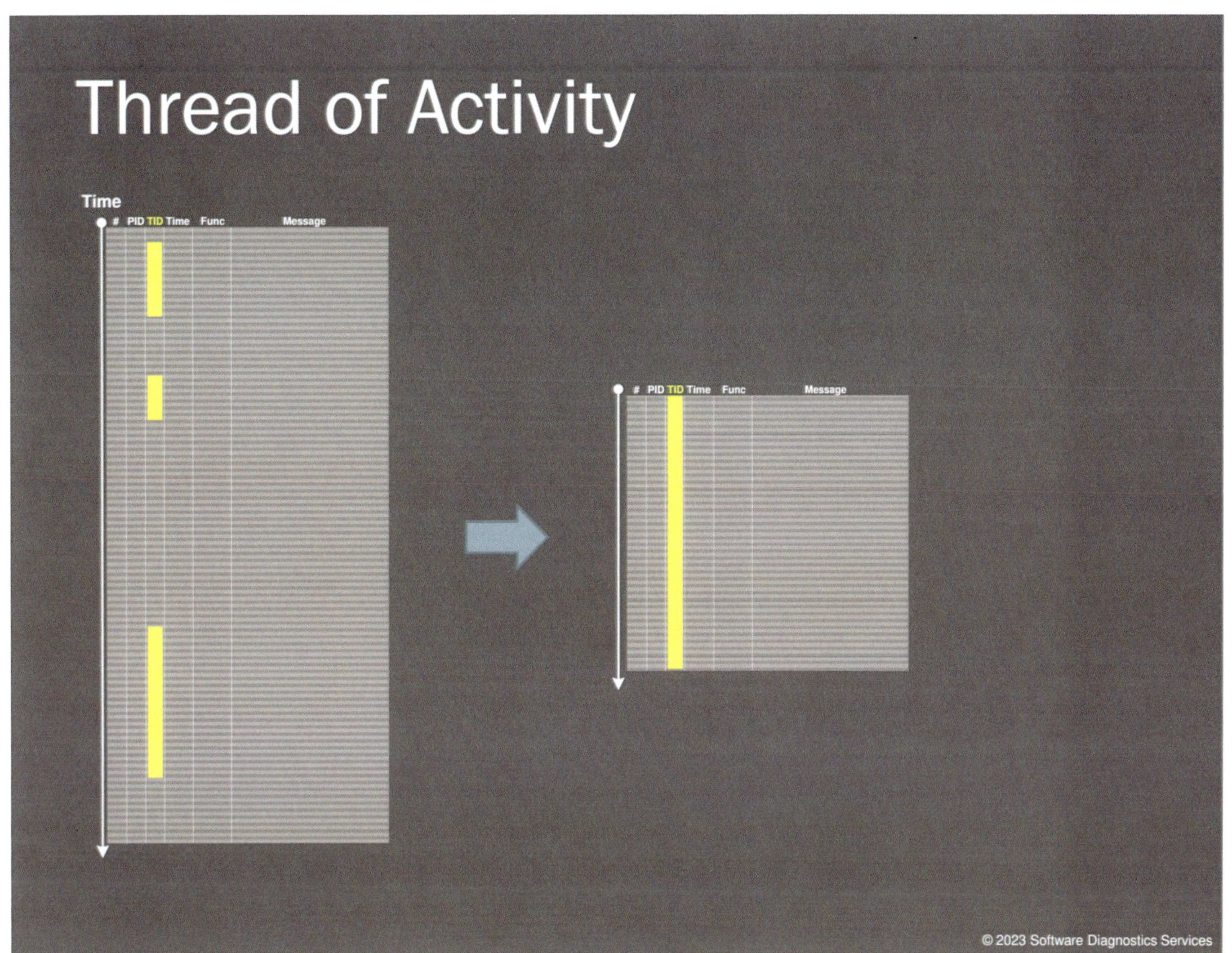

This pattern means trace messages associated with a particular TID. When we see a suspicious message, we select its current thread and investigate what happened in this process and the thread before.

Adjoint Thread of Activity

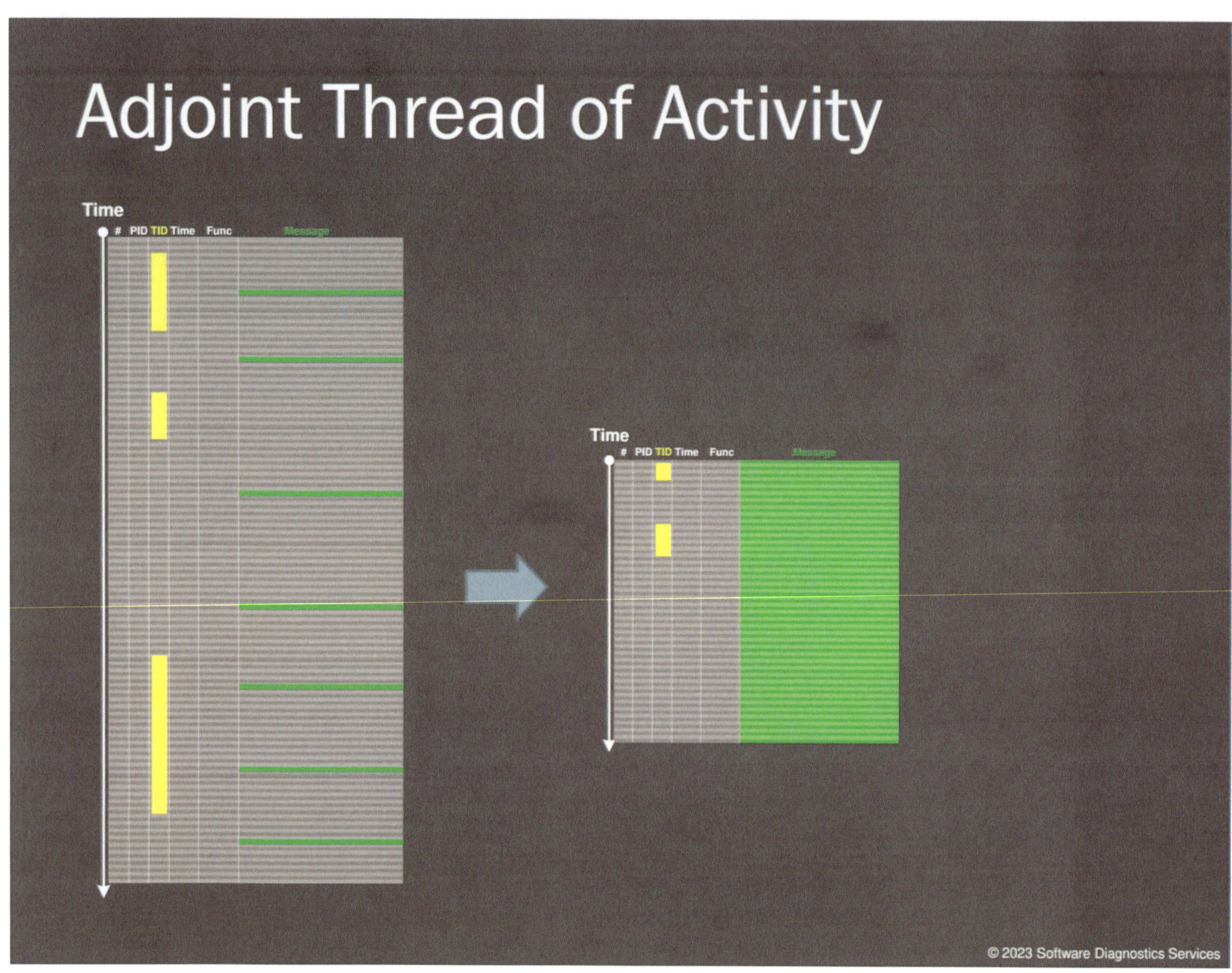

Adjoint Thread is an extension of **Thread of Activity** pattern. In the picture, we see a log message stream where some messages are coming from specific TID shown in yellow color. Suppose we are interested in some specific network operation or registry or file activity, or process name. Then, it is possible to filter such messages and form an adjoint thread of activity for further pattern analysis.

Activity Region

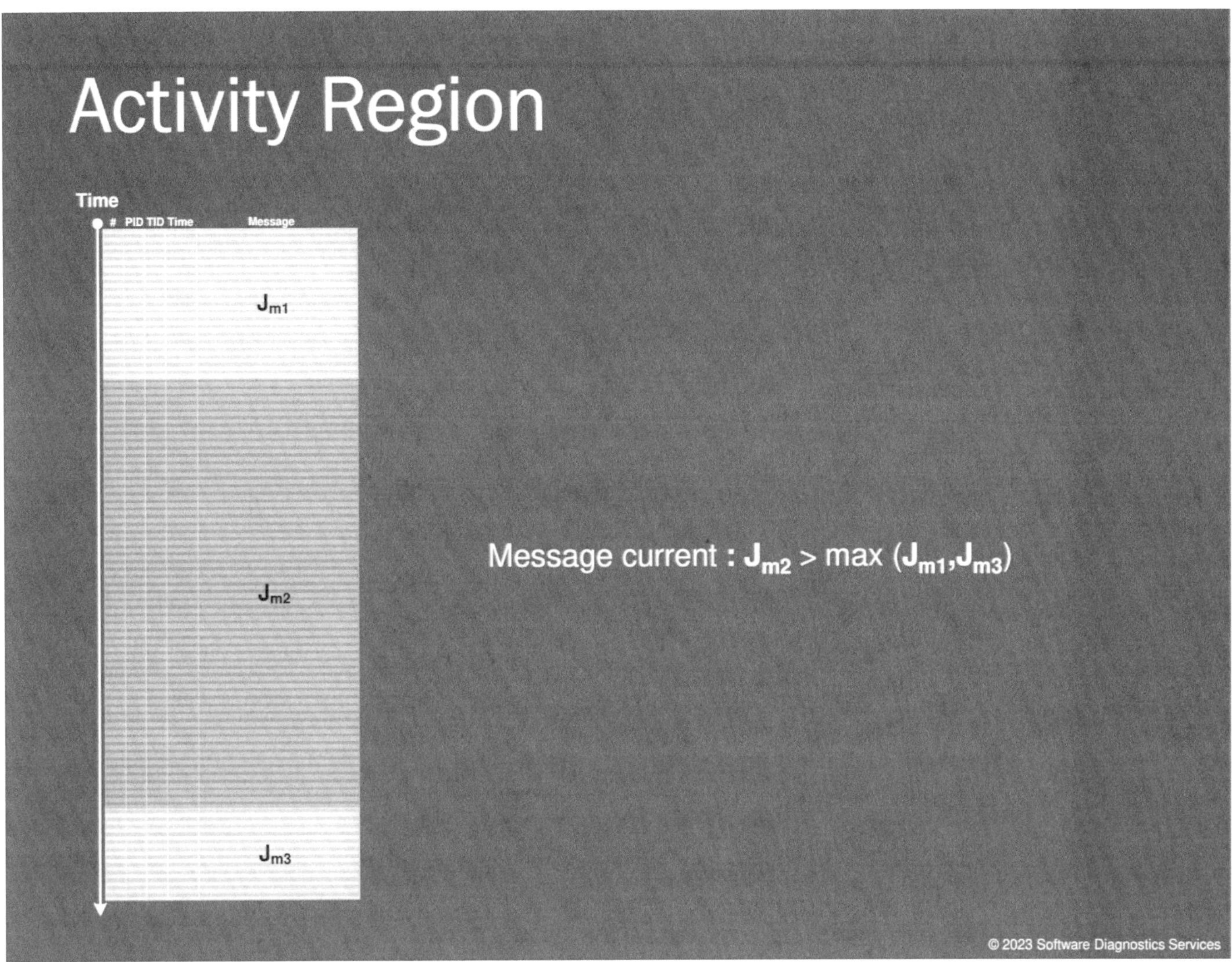

Basically, it is a region of log message stream messages related semantically or syntactically. Of course, it is all relative and dependent on analysis goals. For example, when looking at long traces with millions of messages, we can see regions of activity where **Message Current** (J_m, msg/s) is much higher than in surrounding temporal regions. Another example is a sudden network activity region.

Glued Activity

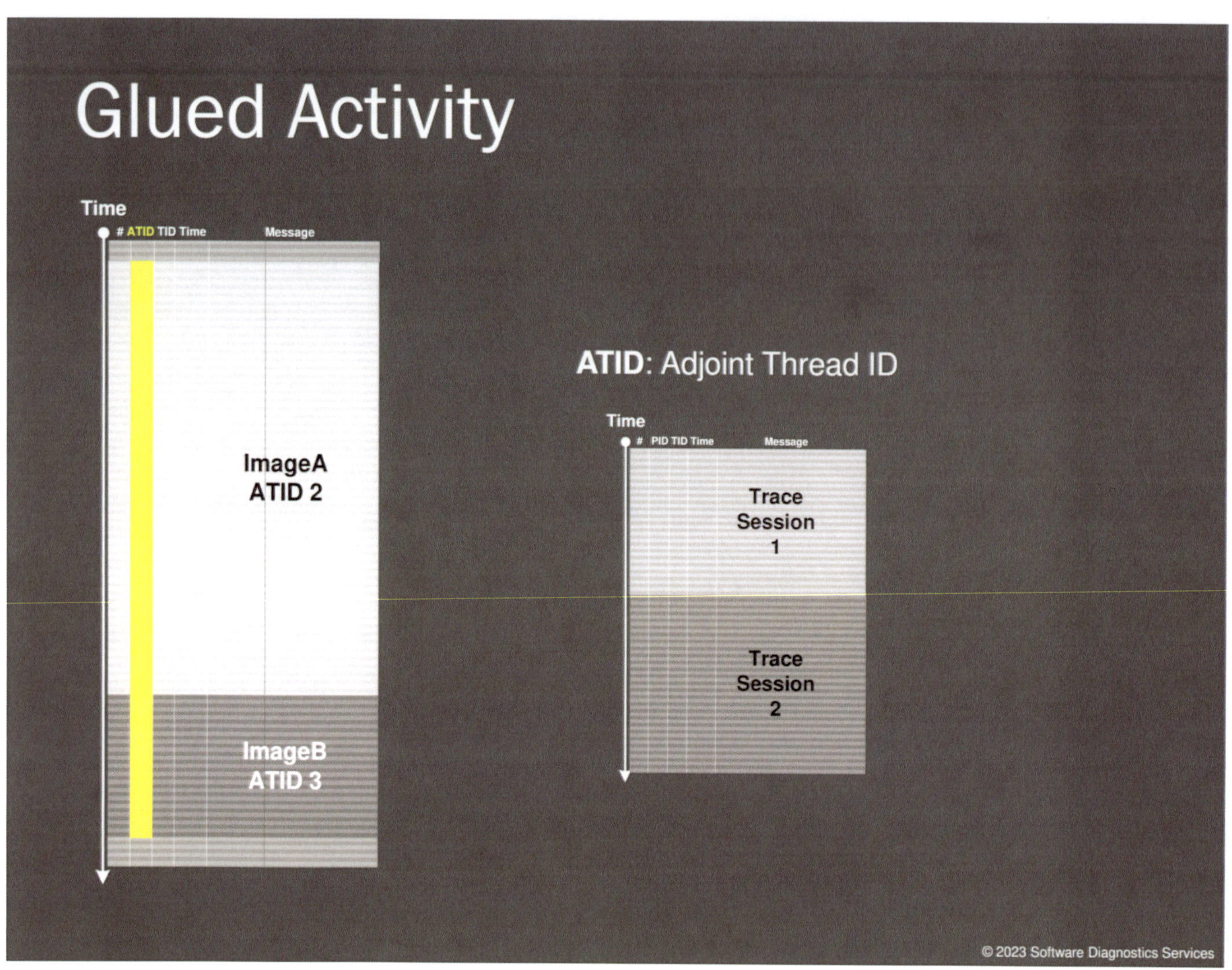

Examples here include log messages from different processes having the same **Adjoint Thread ID,** such as the same operation name or network address. Another example is all messages coming from processes sharing the same name or even, in general, periodic logging sessions appended to the end of the same log file.

Break-in Activity

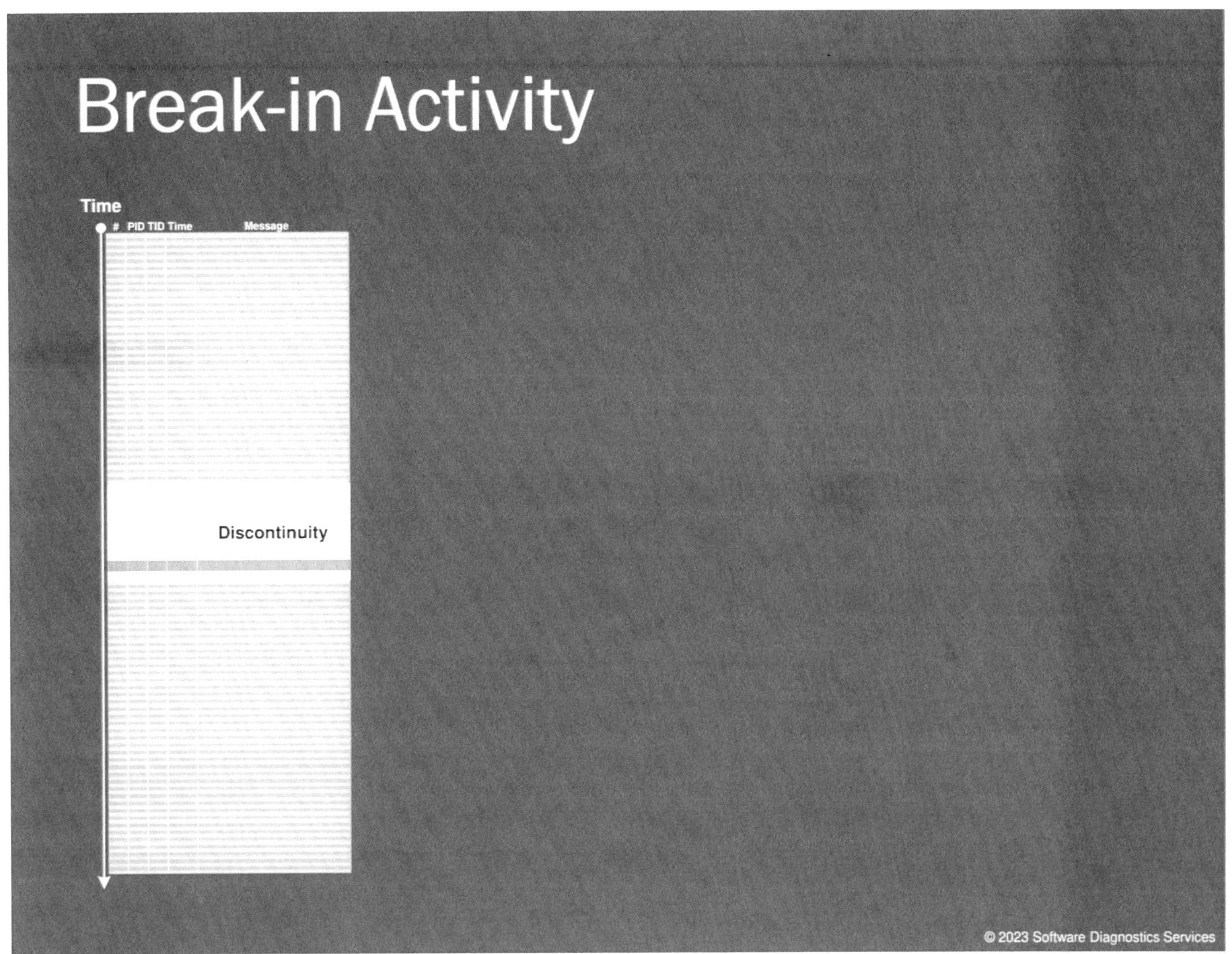

This pattern covers a message or a set of messages that surface just before the end of **Discontinuity** (a temporal gap) of some **Thread of Activity** or **Adjoint Thread**. For example, a silent process suddenly starts some network activity.

Data Flow

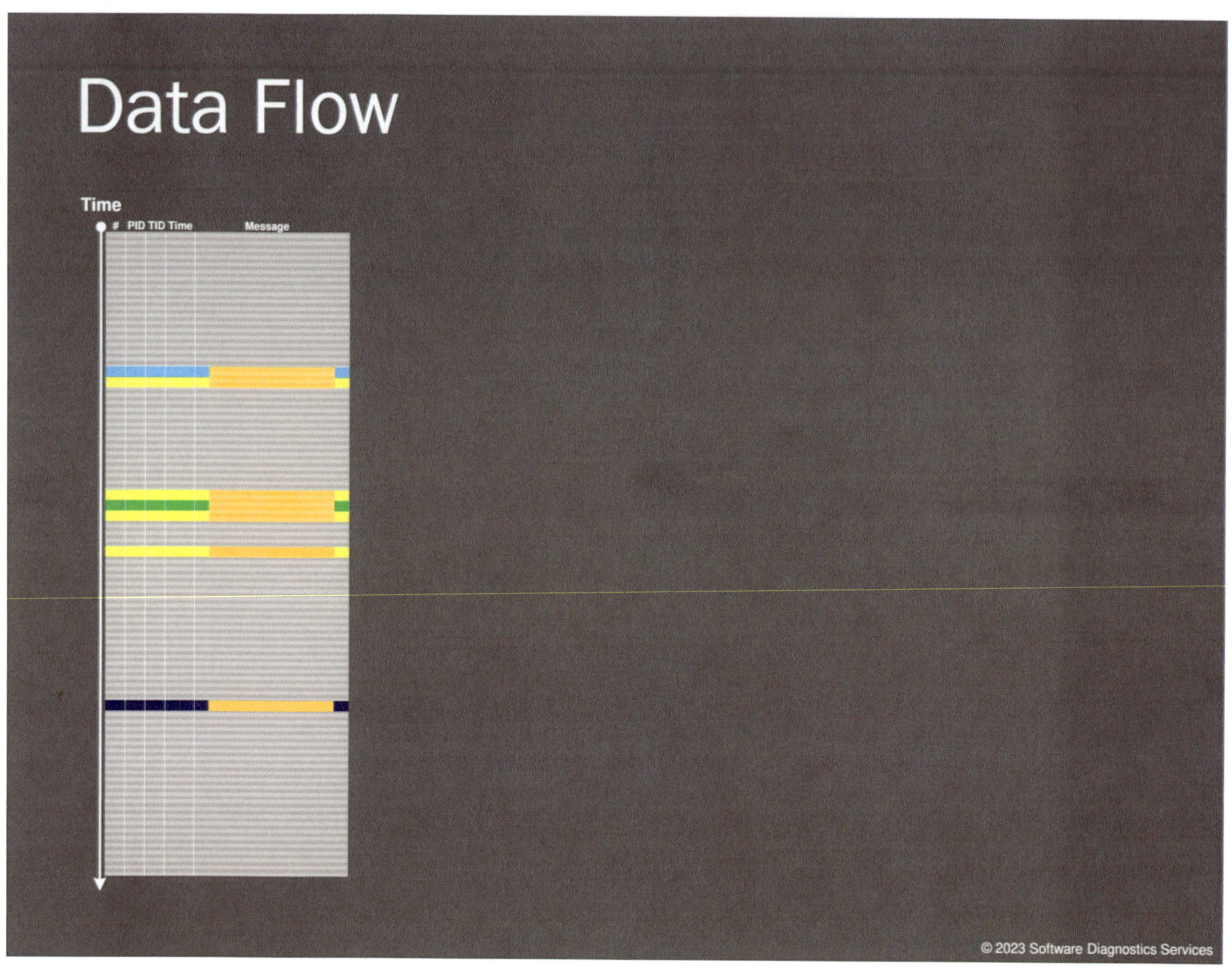

If trace messages contain some character or formatted data passed from module to module or between threads and processes, it is possible to trace that data and form a **Data Flow** "thread" similar to **Adjoint Thread of Activity**. However, for **Data Flow**, we may have completely different message types.

Message Patterns

- Significant Event
- Defamiliarizing Effect
- Anchor Messages
- Diegetic Messages
- Message Change
- Message Invariant
- UI Message
- Original Message
- Implementation Discourse
- Opposition Messages
- Linked Messages
- Gossip
- Counter Value
- Abnormal Value
- Message Context
- Marked Messages
- Incomplete History
- Message Interleave
- Fiber Bundle

The sixth block of patterns includes message patterns or patterns at the level of an individual message.

Significant Event

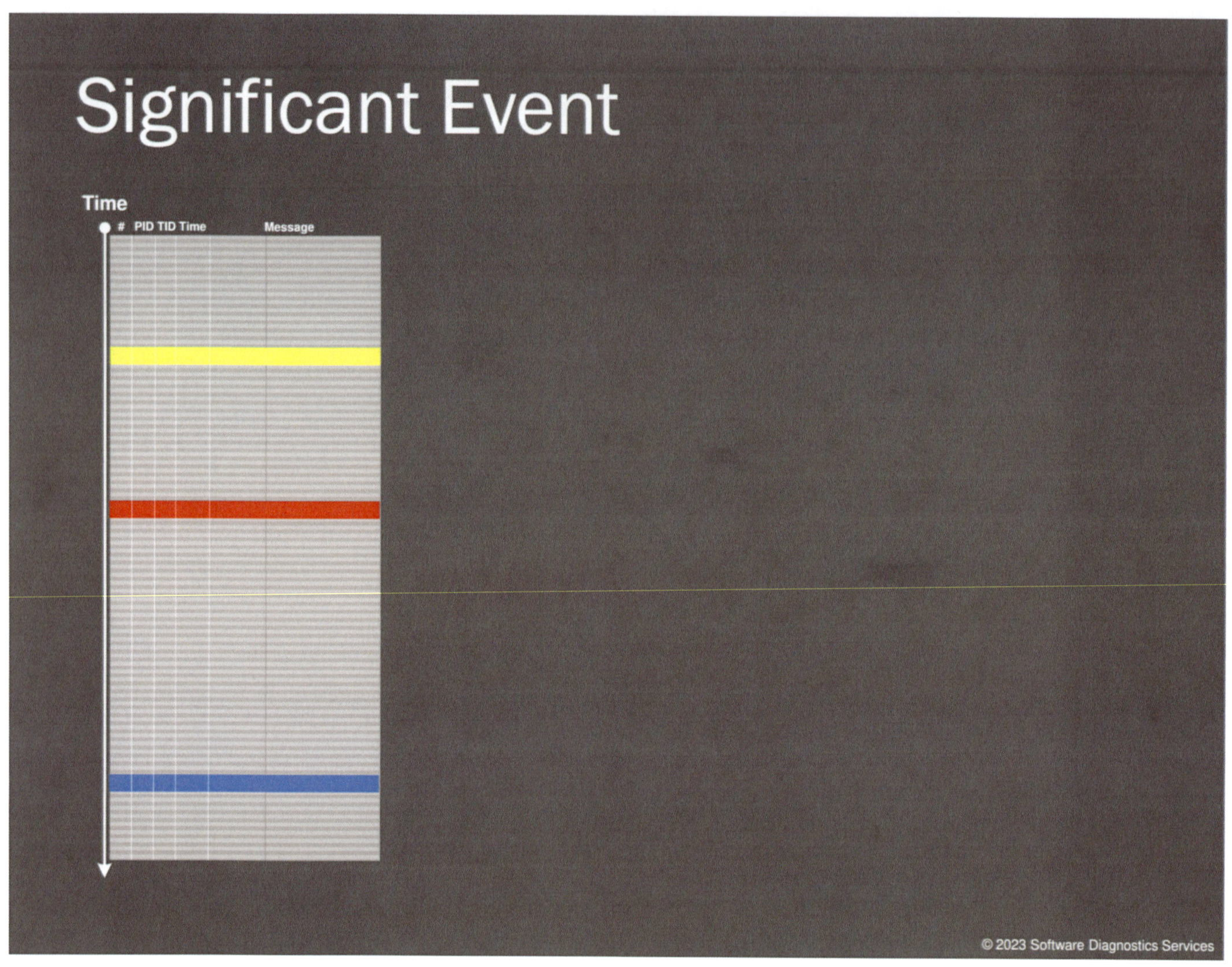

When looking at software traces and logs and doing either a search for or just scrolling certain messages have our attention immediately. We call them **Significant Events**. For malware analysis, any suspicious message, such as updating specific registry keys or creation of a popup window where we don't expect it would count as a significant event.

Defamiliarizing Effect

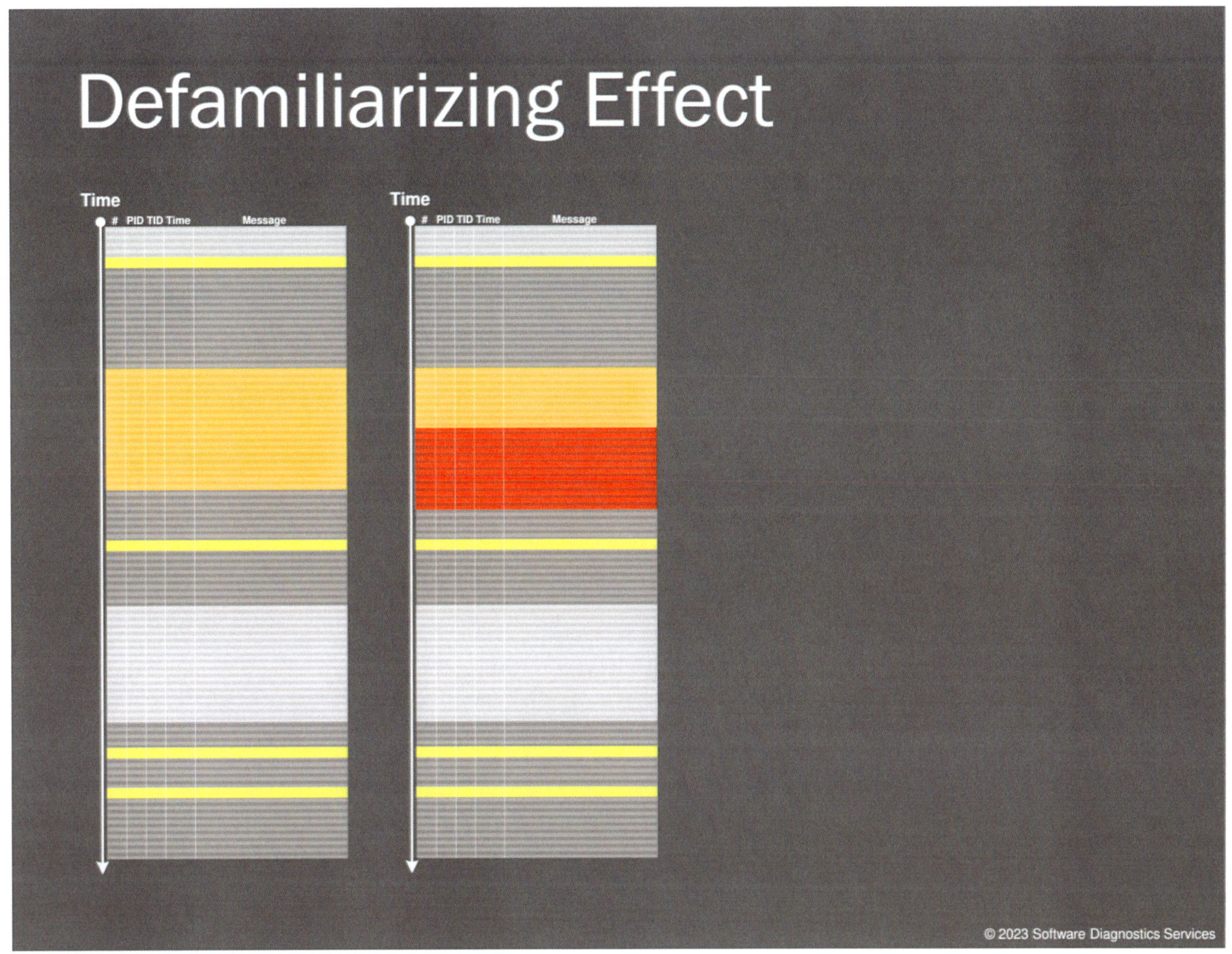

This pattern is about sudden unfamiliar trace statements across the familiar landscape of **Characteristic Blocks** and **Activity Regions**. On the left, we see familiar traces, and on the right, a new trace from an incident system.

Abnormal Value

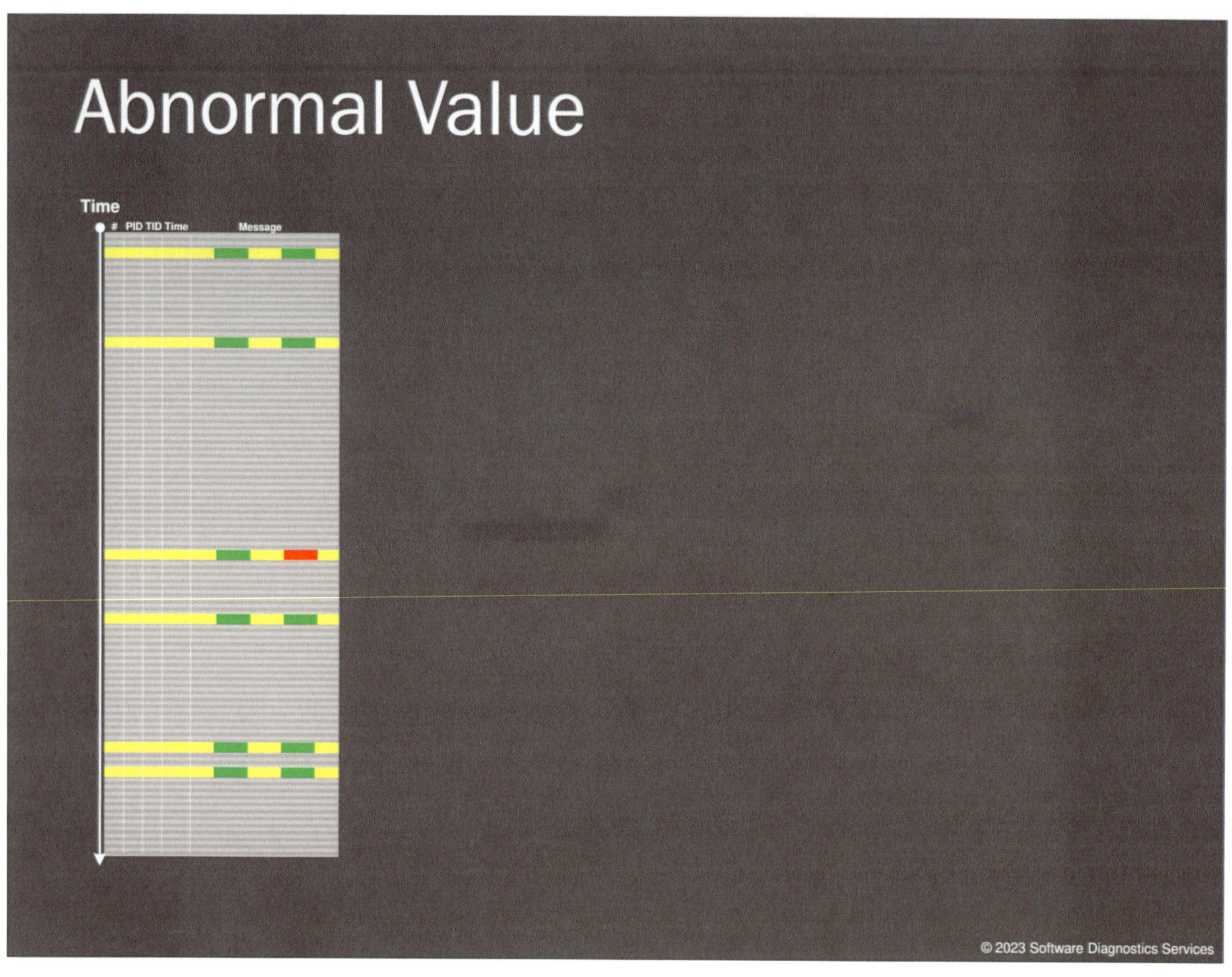

This pattern is about abnormal or unexpected values in a software trace or log, such as a network address outside the expected range.

Marked Messages

Annotated messages:

```
network activity [+]
process A launched [+]
process B launched [-]
process A exited [-]
```

[+] activity is present in a trace
[-] activity is undetected or not present

This pattern groups trace messages based on having some feature or property. For example, marked messages may point to some domain of software activity. Unmarked messages include all other messages that don't say anything about such activities or messages that say explicitly that no such activity has occurred. We can annotate any log after analysis to compare it with a **Master Trace** pattern (which is a normally expected trace corresponding to the normal system).

Fiber Bundle

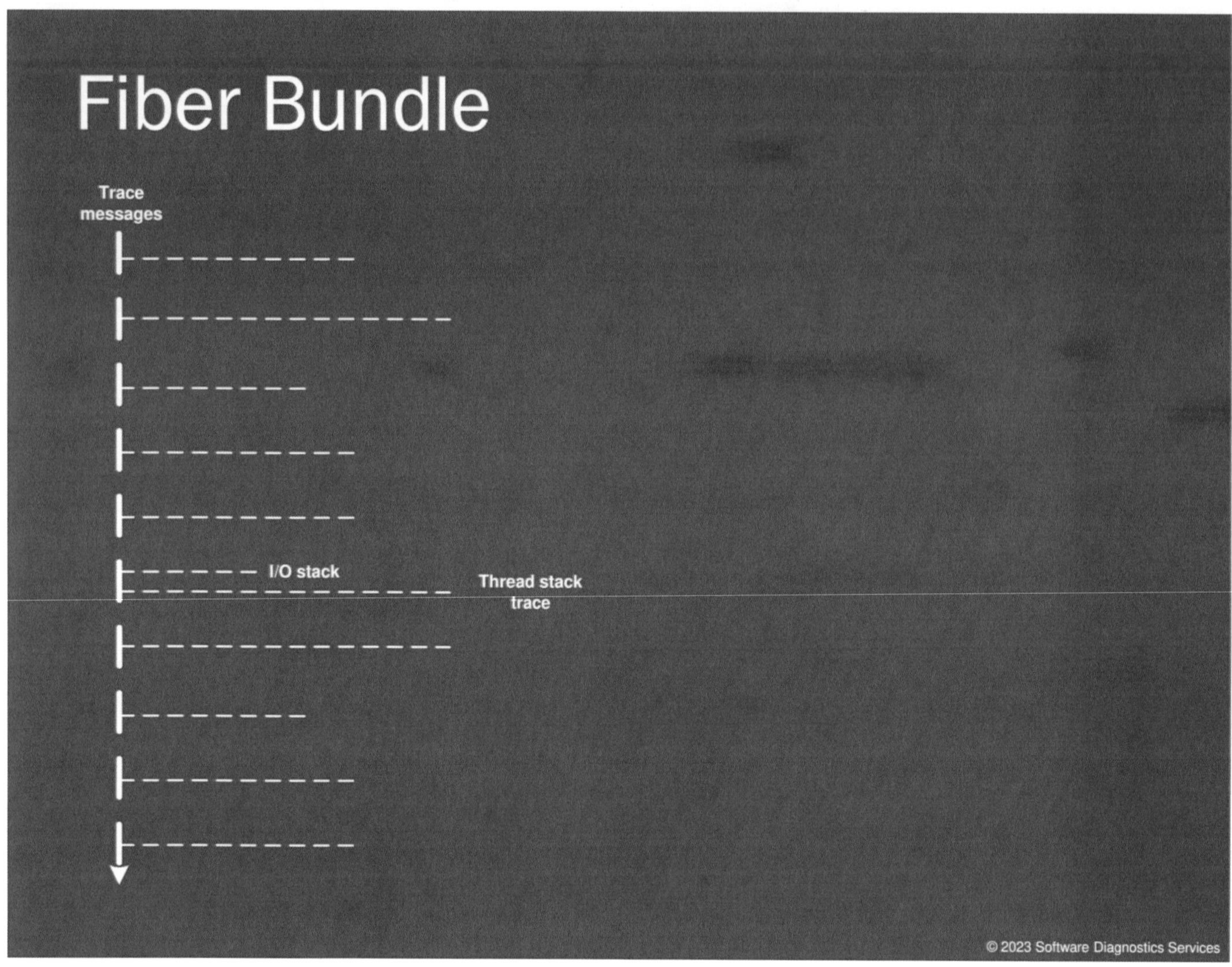

Modern software log recording, visualization, and analysis tools provide stack traces associated with log messages. We can consider stack traces as software logs as well and, in a more general case, bundle them together (or attach them as fibers) to a base software log. For example, a log message that mentions an I/O request packet can have its I/O stack attached together with a thread stack trace with function calls leading to a function that emits the log message.

Block Patterns

- Macrofunction
- Periodic Message Block
- Intra-Correlation

The seventh block is about patterns related to message aggregates or message blocks.

Periodic Message Block

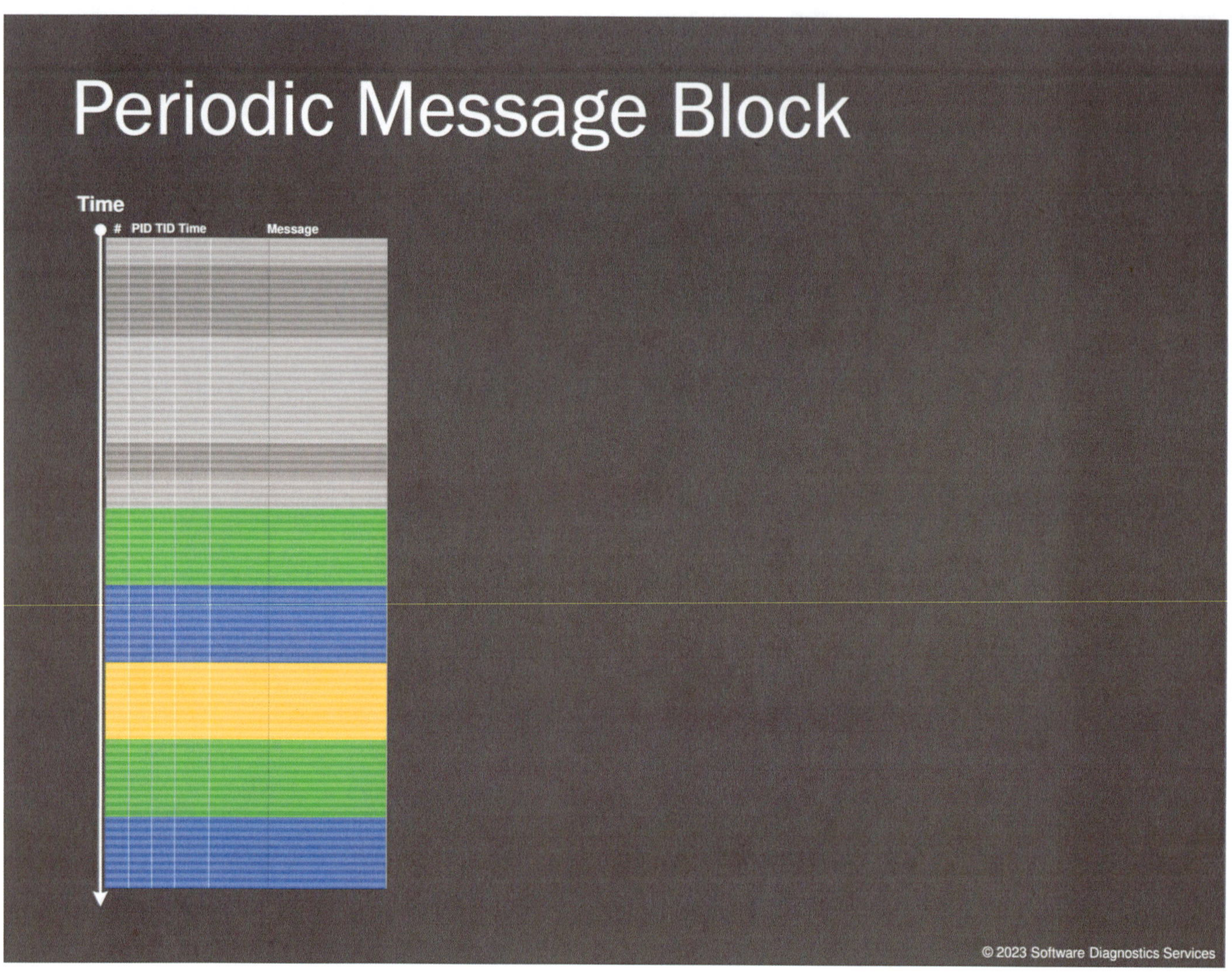

Periodic Message Block is an obvious pattern, for example, repeated network activity messages that are usually grouped together, so I don't provide any further comments here.

Trace Set Patterns

- Master Trace
- Bifurcation Point
- Inter-Correlation
- Relative Density
- News Value
- Impossible Trace
- Split Trace

The eighth block contains patterns for trace sets when we have several software logs.

Master Trace

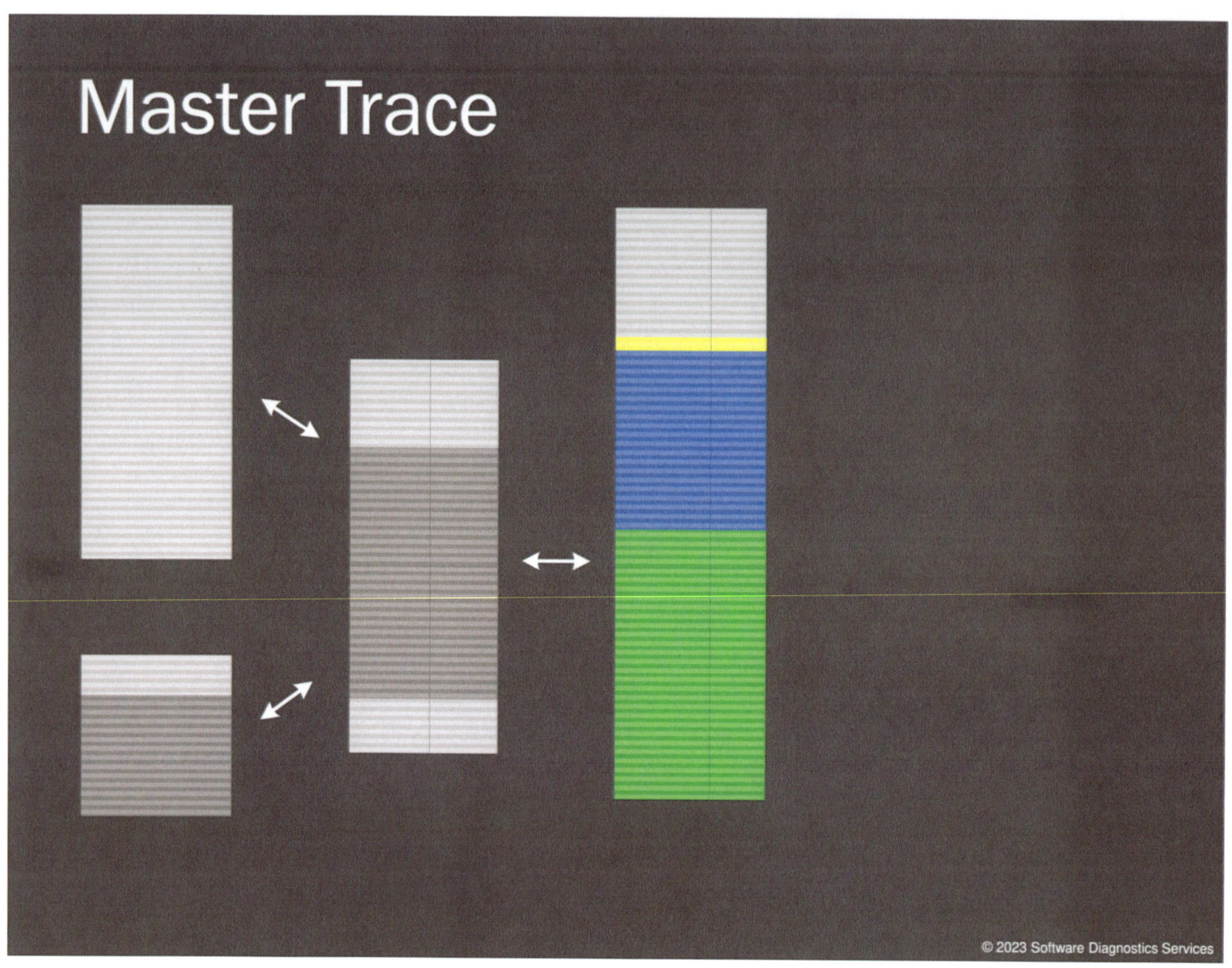

When reading and analyzing software logs, we always compare them to a **Master Trace,** a standard log corresponding to a normal, incident-free use case.

Inter-Correlation

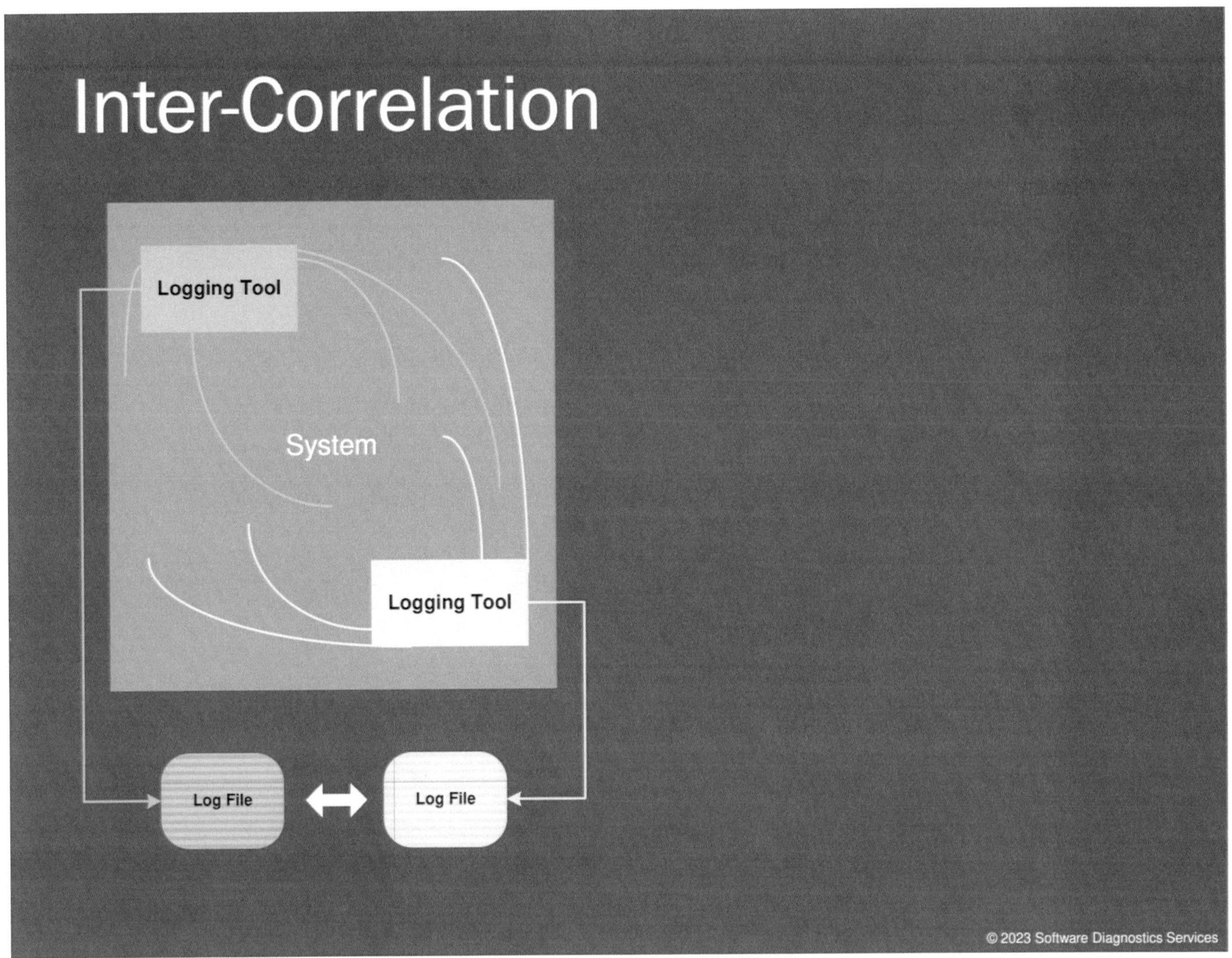

This pattern involves several logs from possibly different logging tools recorded (most commonly) at the same time or during an overlapping time interval. However, the purpose of using different logging tools is to cover events more completely. One of the examples we can provide here is when we have a **Discontinuity**, a gap in one trace, and its interval events are covered by a different tool, or we need to trace network activity more thoroughly in addition to file and registry activity.

Impossible Trace

Although rarely (at least for myself) but it happens that when we look at an execution trace and then say it's an **Impossible Trace**. For example, we see on the trace fragment on the left of this slide that the function *foo* had been called. However, if we look at the corresponding source code on the right, we would see that something is missing: the function *bar* must have been called with its own set of trace messages we don't see in the trace. Here we might suspect that the runtime code was being modified, perhaps by patching. We can also suspect local buffer overflows that led to a wrong return address skipping the code with expected tracing statements.

Grand Unification

- Narrative and Trace

$$N: T \rightarrow M$$

- Generalized Narrative and Trace

$$GN: A \rightarrow M$$

$$GN_3 \circ GN_2 \circ GN_1: M \rightarrow M \rightarrow M$$

Finally, we show what is forthcoming: a grand unification of software log and memory dump analysis through the generalized narrative. Usually, a narrative is a temporal sequence of events, and in the case of a software trace, we can consider it as small memory fragments ordered by time. However, instead of time, we can use any set as a domain of such mapping and even use memory itself and compose narratives together. We'll not talk more about it now.

Further Reading

- Software Diagnostics Institute
- Debugging.TV / YouTube.com/DebuggingTV / YouTube.com/PatternDiagnostics
- Software Trace and Memory Dump Analysis
- Pattern-Driven Software Diagnostics
- Systemic Software Diagnostics
- Pattern-Based Software Diagnostics
- Philosophy of Software Diagnostics
- Theoretical Software Diagnostics
- Software Narratology
- Malnarratives
- Pattern-Oriented Network Trace Analysis
- Accelerated Software Trace Analysis

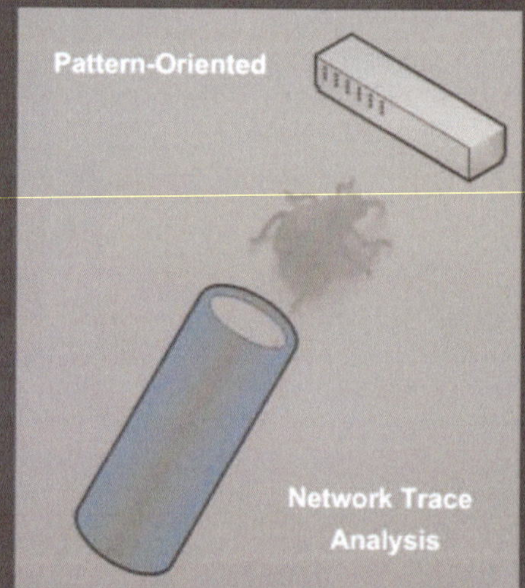

Here are some links for further reading. All log analysis patterns are briefly described on the Software Diagnostics Institute website. They are also available in the edited form in Memory Dump Analysis Anthology volumes starting from volume 3. Also, there is a recorded introduction to Software Narratology and even an accelerated training course.

Software Diagnostics Institute:
https://www.dumpanalysis.org

Software Trace and Memory Dump Analysis:
https://www.dumpanalysis.org/STMDA-book

Pattern-Driven Software Diagnostics:
https://www.dumpanalysis.org/introduction-pattern-driven-diagnostics

Systemic Software Diagnostics:
https://www.dumpanalysis.org/introduction-systemic-software-diagnostics

Pattern-Based Software Diagnostics:
https://www.dumpanalysis.org/introduction-pattern-based-software-diagnostics

Philosophy of Software Diagnostics
https://www.dumpanalysis.org/introduction-philosophy-software-diagnostics

Theoretical Software Diagnostics
http://www.patterndiagnostics.com/theoretical-software-diagnostics-book

Software Narratology
https://www.dumpanalysis.org/10-years-software-narratology

Malnarratives
http://www.dumpanalysis.org/malnarratives

Pattern-Oriented Network Trace Analysis
https://www.dumpanalysis.org/pattern-oriented-network-trace-analysis

Accelerated Software Trace Analysis
https://www.patterndiagnostics.com/accelerated-software-trace-analysis-part1

Historical Reference

Volume 15 is planned for 2023

Memory Dump Analysis Anthology:
https://www.patterndiagnostics.com/mdaa-volumes

Alphabetical Reference

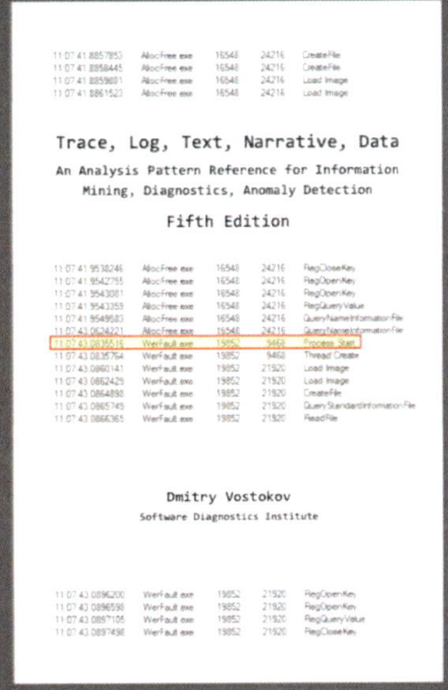

Trace, Log, Text, Narrative, Data: An Analysis Pattern Reference for Information Mining, Diagnostics, Anomaly Detection, Fifth Edition:
https://www.patterndiagnostics.com/trace-log-analysis-pattern-reference

A Guide to Learning Software Trace and Log Analysis Patterns
https://www.educative.io/courses/guide-learning-software-trace-log-analysis-patterns